From the Edge of the Marsh

From the Edge of the Marsh

Jeff Keene II

WordCrafts Press

To my father, Jeffrey "Peachy" C. Keene II

His idea of an afterlife always involved being at the bay house on a beautiful summer day spending time with his family and friends.

Contents

998 Scow Creek post–Hurricane Gloria.

The bay houses in the Town of Hempstead have a long history that starts in the 19th century, when baymen created protected shelters while harvesting oysters, clams, finfish, and waterfowl. The first structures were made using mudsills, a sophisticated system of creating a platform for the bay house. Today, the bay houses stand on pilings as marshlands recede.

In *From the Edge of the Marsh*, Jeff Keene II recalls the heyday of the bay houses when hundreds stretched across the town, owned by baymen, "water rats," and recreational fishermen and their families. Keene's personal memoir is a testament to the local knowledge bay house owners inherited from previous generations of baymen and bay house owners. In many ways, Keene introduces us to the cultural traditions of this unique group—stories and practices passed down from generation to generation. Keene introduces us to the Combs family of Freeport, who have worked the bay for over 200 years. Their bay house survived but was severely damaged by Superstorm Sandy in 2012. Today, it is being rebuilt so it can serve future generations of the family.

This book provides a personal perspective on maintaining the bay house, and the traditions of hunting, fishing, and playing practical jokes. You will find humorous stories alongside tales of close calls on the bay. These voices give us an intimate entry into this unique world. *Long Island Traditions* is proud to share this world with you.

~Nancy Solomon, Historian and former Executive Director
Long Island Traditions

The following is based upon an excerpt from an opening day duck hunting trip recorded on a cassette tape by the author's father in 1977 when the author was just seven years old:

Mush, wrinkled and tanned hide owner of 998 Scow Creek and legendary bayman, sat at the end of a Formica table. You know the ones. Green glittery flecks on an off-white background edged entirely in chrome. This one had seen better years and was probably a hand-me-down from someone's grandparents. After listening for a time to the colorful conversation in the bay house, he remarked in his gravelly voice, "Hey, maybe we could make a movie here."

To which his friend and bay house caretaker Jack replied, "Imagine the six of us in Hollywood."

Mush cleared his throat the best he could. It sounded like a chainsaw engine turning over. "Well, I'll tell ya. With all the experiences, and sayings, and stuff, and different boats—if you could take notes, of who said things and whatnot, and wrote a book, they could really make some money."

Charley fixed his wire-rimmed glasses and brushed back his thin gray hair. "That's right."

A contemplative look grew on Jeff's bearded face while he mused on the subject. He then tilted his head as a dog does when hearing a strange noise. "How do you write the sound of a fart?"

The company erupted in laughter.

Introduction
A Bay House's Perspective

998 Scow Creek, pre-Hurricane Gloria (1985) – The World Trade Center Twin Towers 23-miles away on the western horizon.

They once called me a barn. Can you believe that? Before severing my sturdy poles to separate me from dry land. Before dragging my dusty frame onto a barge, towing me across the shallow salty bay, all those years ago. Never had I imagined what waited on the marshes of Long Island's south shore for this former hulking cowshed. A simple garage, now destined for a new and glorious adventure.

Boards creaked, echoing my escalating fears. The briny water licked my mud-stained foundation driving fat spiders to scurry up to the rafters. At least it had the pleasant effect of ridding the termites from my sills. The entire nest—eggs, soldiers, and workers—floated off in a thick mat of writhing paleness. Food for a myriad of fish and crabs below. I missed the larger animals that once shared my interior. Their earthy smells lingered in the crevices and knots of my wood, soon to be replaced by new scents: fried eel, suntan lotion, and gunpowder solvent.

For all I knew, they towed me out here to the middle of nowhere to be sawn into firewood or scuttled like some outdated, overused fishing vessel. Destined to spend eternity at the bottom of the estuary slowly encrusted in sessile barnacles and dissected by gnawing shipworms and sponges.

But when they lifted my shifting edifice onto the muddy grassland, I knew my days of being useful had not ended. The long timbers and thick creosote poles supporting me several feet above the sucking mud would serve, along with my walls, windows, and roof, to entertain, protect, inspire, and even corrupt those who spent just a few hours here. They now called me a 'bay house' and even blessed me with an address all my own: 998 Scow Creek.

But my newfound location came with its own demanding concerns. On the mainland, I didn't worry about tropical hurricanes or arctic nor'easters washing me away. No one broke my aged windows to ravage and steal. Seagulls didn't drop quahog clams on my asphalt shingles then defecate on my white paint while devouring the rewards of their clever predation.

Nevertheless, I sit here now, exposed to the elements. No foliage to shade the blistering summer sun or divert the fracturing winter snow. I stand bare on a treeless plain, dominated by *Spartina* grass, once called "salt hay" by local cow farmers, and succulent glasswort, used today as a delicacy in the salads of fine restaurants. Here, the rising tide greets me, then ebbs away with comforting regularity.

I found unexpected joy in being a bay house.

Laughter and tears filled my airy interior. Families celebrated birthdays, anniversaries, and holidays near my warm glowing hearth, around my broad decks, and on my floating docks. Friends grew close, and some grew even closer. People now used me for much more than animal husbandry or storing vehicles. I was now one of them. A member of their inner circle, so close they fell in love with me and what I stood for.

Freedom.

Freedom from the confined spaces and concrete surfaces of a

sprawling New York City suburbia. Freedom from the monotony of a 9-to-5 workday, overbearing bosses, and stressful highway commutes. Freedom to retreat to a place where time had stopped a hundred years ago allowing pioneer life to prevail to this day.

This blessed perch, this stationary vantage point, gave me a perspective only a gifted few would learn to appreciate through the years. It was here, from the edge of the marsh, where it all took place.

I

Boats & Bay Houses

Not every Islander owns a boat. And for that, I am thankful. Their careless piloting as they barrel full speed down the buoy-marked channel makes me wish my caretakers had mounted a cannon on my deck. Their passage sends an incessant barrage of wake crests that pummel the fragile mud bank, the only protection between the water and my tenuous foundation.

Piece by mushy piece, regardless of the tendrils of *Spartina* grass roots grasping the mud with microscopic fibers, the marsh erodes

The author as a teen in the 1980s showing off a summer founder caught from his grandfather's pole on a garvey floating in Scow Creek.

into the bay. It fouls the water, chokes the wildlife, and fills the very channels those people rely on for safe, deep navigation. They only hurt themselves with this reckless behavior. An ecosystem existing since the last glaciers retreated and deposited Long Island thousands of years ago, decimated in less than one lifetime by ignorant human activity. An ecological disaster due to a lack of patience and an even greater lack of education.

But not all who travel these waters are so irresponsible. Those who care for me ferry boatloads of concrete blocks, construction debris, and bushel bags filled with clam shells from the mainland. By placing these breakwaters at my feet, they help to prevent erosion and preserve me for future generations.

I continue to exist, teach, and inspire today because of these new custodians, who learn young that you only love what you fear might be lost.

One

THREE MEN IN A TUB

*T*he boys who grew up visiting the bay house sought mischief, as most boys do, with a frequency unrivaled by many Long Island children in the 1970s and '80s. Could they be considered rednecks in such proximity to densely populated New York City? Clamming, fishing, swimming, hunting, and exploring the wilds of the south shore's salt marshes kept them busy weekday afternoons, weekends, and all summer long. And all within view of the hazy Manhattan skyline on the western horizon. The lessons they learned would never be known by those raised from landlubber parents who favored swimming pools over sandbars and movie theatres over meandering tides.

The marsh lay ripe with discoveries. Mosquito ditches crossed the surface of the salty meadow in parallel lines, dug in the first half of the twentieth century by the Army Corps of Engineers. And

John Combs III, Jeff Keene II, Michael J. Combs, c. 1978 – The Point Lookout water tower can be seen in the distance.

natural saltwater *cricks* carved their way in serpentine paths through the islands, often severing those manmade ditches. The result, a multitude of lesser islands diced from the original. Small, often deep, and inconspicuous holes pockmarked the flat and treeless terrain.

Fiddler crab and muskrat dens lined the creeks, mats of dark green translucent sea lettuce and wracks of brown seaweed called *pop grass* clung to the banks at low tide, and fresh water trickled from a rusty iron pipe into a stark white, clawfoot bathtub.

This last displaced phenomenon fascinated three young boys on an otherwise common summer day. They always knew about the artesian well, a quarter mile southeast of the bay house, where thirsty birds often drank their fill. It once served the kitchen hand pump in a former neighboring bay house now swept away by an unnamed storm years ago or ravaged by fire. The boys themselves had drunk from this deep aquifer lifeline on more than one occasion. The water tasted of metal, but anyone who has drank well water from a clean source can attest to its health benefits. Just as long as the boys didn't drink from the tub itself.

Besides, it resembled a boat just too closely.

After wrestling the old cistern from the marsh, being careful not to damage the pipe, they pushed it into the crick.

"Three men in tub," they exclaimed, and piled in one by one, laughing at their self-perceived ingenuity and the prospect of using it to float across the channel.

The first two boys, cousins John and Jeff, had no problem paddling the improvised craft with their hands into the openness of Scow Creek. But when the third and oldest boy, Mike, managed to climb aboard, water sloshed over the edges until gravity overcame buoyancy.

Their makeshift vessel sank faster than a block of wet concrete. It's final vision of the sun that had bathed it for decades ended with a *kerplunk* as it penetrated the depths of the channel.

The boys hollered and laughed, all the while disregarding any wrongdoing they'd done. After swimming to shore and traipsing through the marsh back to the bay house, they soon moved on to other distractions.

Thirty minutes later, their Uncle Mush arrived on his

nineteen-foot fiberglass boat, the *Kingfish*. "You know what those boys did?" he yelled as he climbed onto the bay house's floating dock. His gruff voice even more harsh than normal. It matched the skin on his face, being roughly carved by decades of cigarettes and rye whiskey.

Apparently, the bay house owner across the crick had watched the boys in awe while relaying the heinous scheme to Mush via CB radio. He had received a play-by-play account.

After hearing the complaint, John and Mike's father, Jack, gathered up the boys and gave them a talking to. Without a doubt, Mike received the harshest punishment, having been the eldest in the trio of troublemakers. He was tasked with accompanying his father in a vain attempt to find the sunken tub.

The boys learned a valuable lesson that day. Jack explained that the tub served as a watering hole for the natural fauna, including the waterfowl their family hunted every season, and held sentimental value as the last remnant to the historical bay house it once served.

Thinking about consequences before acting is a skill often learned only by longsuffering and repeated disappointment. And through all the experiences, it's the grace of God that allows us to move on from mistakes and become ever wiser because of them.

George "Uncle Mush" Carman - Original lessee of 998 Scow Creek.

Two

THE POTBELLY STOVE

*W*inters at the bay house could numb the skin and warm the heart. Whether hunting or celebrating holidays, the potbelly stove sat as the centerpiece during it all. Cooking, boiling water, drying clothes, and providing life-giving heat when the west wind *hawk* blew hard against the whistling windowpanes made maintenance of the stove and its fire a primary and constant task. The sound of escaping gases from within the wood's fibrous grains filled the bay house with a crackling and hissing to forever remind us of the comfort and security provided by the ferrous hearth.

The stove wasn't always the classic stout centerpiece most country cabins are thought to possess. Necessity is the mother of invention. So any improvement on a system of life-giving warmth needed to be tested for efficiency and ease of deployment.

At one time at 998 Scow Creek, a system of two interconnected fifty-five-gallon steel drums, one situated above the other within an iron frame, served to capture more warmth as hot smoke traveled through the flue and out the galvanized chimney pipe. The second drum radiated heat into the living space rather than letting it escape from the chimney and into the universe beyond.

In any scenario, a pile of sawn and chopped firewood lasted only so long into the winter season. And a stand of lumber wasn't going to cut itself into suitable pieces without frost nipped noses and splintered fingers.

Every time a group of duck hunters left the bay house, it was typical to leave behind a volunteer to tend the fire and prepare the next meal. This time, that task fell upon Jack. As a head of the bay house's ownership and upkeep, everyone had faith in his abilities with both responsibilities. Now, the conveyor belt and assembly line had been invented nearly a century before when Henry Ford built his Model-Ts. So putting the idea into practice out here seemed only logical.

The sun rose, and the morning hunt ended. Growling stomachs and decreased waterfowl activity forced the men back to the welcoming smells of a warm fire, bacon, and griddle cakes. As they entered the bay house, a most curious sight welcomed them.

An eight-foot-long plank extended from the potbelly stove's open door. The non-burning end rested steadily on a dining room chair. Jack sat on the couch with one foot slowly pushing the chair across the linoleum floor closer to the stove, inching the wood into the fire. Jack's ingenious plan to avoid extra work had the unpleasant side effect of filling the upstairs sleeping quarters with smoke.

The guys quickly filled their plates and enjoyed breakfast outside on the deck that morning, regardless of the chilly air. Afterward, they turned their efforts from hunting to cutting wood to prevent another bright idea about saving time or increasing efficiency from rearing its ugly head.

Three

Wood from a Woodless Plain

*T*he wood pile eventually ran low, and new sources proved scarce on a treeless, salty plain. The idea of chopping wood on land, loading it up on the boat, carting it all the way across the bay, and unloading it onto the deck at the bay house never caught on. So, where did all the firewood come from?

The estuary is full of diverse lifeforms. It's known as the *ocean's nursery* and is one of the most productive ecosystems on the planet second only to rainforests and coral reefs. Equally varied are the topographical features found there, ranging from sand dunes, tidal pools, algae mats, and shell piles created from years of seagulls dropping clams from above. But nothing matches the myriad of flotsam and jetsam found washed up onto the banks and into the reeds by high tides.

Many of these items were found useful: boat bumpers, lengths of rope, seat cushions, toys, fishing gear, and hunting decoys. Even an occasional boat could be found floundering in some backwater crick or deep in the tall grass, ripe for scavenging stainless steel cleats and other hardware. But nothing was more plentiful than wood. Driftwood, plywood, planking, and poles. Not one piece of

Turk, the Labrador retriever, gladly returns with a duck to a deck composed of boards from various sources.

new lumber was ever purchased from a hardware store for repairs, nor any trees sacrificed for want of fuel.

The site of a fourteen-foot garvey bursting at the seams with *marsh wood* as water lapped over its sides brought joy to the guys waiting at the bay house. It meant the potbelly stove would continue to provide the life-sustaining heat and soul-replenishing warmth so relied upon by its users.

Four

PUMPKIN SEEDS, RAZOR BLADES, & JELLY BOATS

*L*et's make one thing perfectly clear. People cannot access the bay house without a boat. Well, there was this one time, but we'll save that story for another chapter.

All sorts of boats have been either docked or anchored nearby: kayaks and paddleboats, canoes and gheenoes, skiffs, dories, and garveys, motorboats, speedboats, sailboats, and cabin cruisers. Shallowness defined the water during most hours of the day in front of the bay house. Therefore, owners of larger boats required assistance in getting ashore. That's why flat-bottomed boats had historically proven essential in the bay and had also been useful in rescuing those who ran aground while failing to navigate around the sand bar that laid between the bay house and the navigational channel.

Baymen built garveys with a simple wood frame and marine plywood exterior. Covering the bottom and sides with fiberglass and resin ensured a waterproof seal and an appropriate surface for gliding on the water. These boats typically ranged in length from twelve to twenty-five feet

Jeff "Peachy" Keene Sr. at a bay house on Scow Creek, c. 1984.

and could be used for fishing, clamming, net casting, and a myriad of other activities. They were extremely adaptable and, when covered in lathing and harvested saltmarsh grass, made impressive duck hunting vessels blending into the mud banks with ease.

One year, in the mid-1980s, Mike needed a new garvey. Whether he wanted to save money or was pressed for time, no one may ever know. But the result of his labors produced a diminutive eight-foot masterpiece that, quite possibly, no one had ever seen the likes of before.

On an early fall afternoon, several of the regular bay house attendees, including Jeff "Peachy" Keene Sr., had been summoned to prepare for the upcoming hunting season. Cutting wood, cleaning cobwebs, repairing shingles, and securing loose dock boards took most of their day. Peachy looked west toward Middle Bay upon hearing the distant hum of a small boat engine. Guests often stopped what they were doing to determine what visitor would soon grace them with their presence. A tiny boat skimmed along the surface of the water backlit by the late afternoon sunlight. The vessel barreled around the bend from the north and entered Scow Creek.

Through the spray, not much of the boat's pattern could be made out. It was as if an invisible craft, propelled by some immense force and being piloted by a ghost, made its way across the crick. And it was headed straight for the bay house over puddle-thin water.

As it approached, Peachy stood in awe. He called for others to witness the apparition. "Where're the binoculars? Looks like a razor blade comin' 'cross the bay."

When young Mike finally pulled up to the dock, and the tiny boat came to a halt, only then could they see the reality of what sat before them. The fifty-horsepower Evinrude engine bolted to the transom of that eight-foot garvey forced the bow into the air and the stern into the water. Only at open throttle did the boat plane itself out. At this point, had there been a dozen little people in clown suits pouring out of it onto the dock, it couldn't have been more hilarious.

From then on, the *Razor Blade* became a well-known boat in the area. After its novelty wore off only months later, Mike's father, Jack, forced him to change up the engine to something within safer limits.

James Combs pilots the 'razor blade' toward south Baldwin with Turk,
Jack's Labrador retriever, riding on the bow.

Other infamous boats came and went at the bay house over
the years. But hunting vessels held a particular interest for everyone.
The versatility of their small size, durability, low draft, flat bows, and
non-encumbering height above water made them a commodity few
could live without. If you could fit the boat into smaller cricks, propel
it without noise, and camouflage it, all the better.

The *Pumpkin Seed*, so dubbed by Jack, was just one of those boats.
It resembled a fat *pepita*, in shape and color, if only a pumpkin seed
had a hole on one side for a small insect to sit in while it skidded
across a bowl of water.

Unfortunately, this tiny vessel didn't see much use after its first
season at the bay house. Most of us preferred to hunt with at least
one other person, and the *Pumpkin Seed* sat one lone hunter. Because
it lacked a motor, you could only use it near the bay house, unless
you towed it behind a normal boat. Many of the best hunting spots
were at least ten-minutes away via motorized boat, so convenience
outweighed that level of stealth.

The *Pumpkin Seed* woefully sat tied up to the bay house pilings
for two seasons slowly succumbing to the elements until finally being
released to boat heaven.

The last boat needing mention here is one that should've been memorialized with a plaque. The *Jelly Boat* had once been a fine multi-purpose transport perfect for exploring this environment. Hand-built with unique L-shaped sidewalls allowing for ease of camouflage and a narrow beam for navigating tight saltmarsh channels, it served its owner for over three decades. Through ice, extreme tides, and gale force winds, she held fast. Not bad for a garvey made from spare wood and by a person with little formal training as a shipwright.

John E. Combs Sr. built that boat in the 1950s. By the time the grandkids grew old enough to adopt it in the '80s, saltwater had seeped in from underneath while unbaled freshwater from rains had done so from above. The resulting swollen wood undulated when it rode over waves giving it the alarming appearance of a bowl full of shaken jelly, hence its name.

One of the *Jelly Boat's* final voyages involved Mike, John, and Cousin Jeff. Mike and John were brothers separated by two years of age and twenty degrees of inhibition. Jeff, their first cousin, often joined in their escapades as if he were another sibling.

While preparing this well-seasoned garvey for the fast approaching opening day of duck season, Jack sanctioned the boys with acquiring the saltmarsh grass needed to properly camouflage it and some of their other boats. This grass, called *thatch*, was ripped from the marsh by hand and secured to the decking with strips of lathing. Afterwards, it resembled a thatched straw roof. Neat, tight,

Ricky "Surf" Laudman's duck hunting boat freshly covered in thatch.

and virtually undetectable by waterfowl when properly moored near an embankment, this camouflage was unmatched by any store-bought replacement.

Typically, thatch was collected in bundles and stacked inside the boat for transport to the mainland for installation. The boys succeeded but decided to play a joke on their fathers who waited at the bay house anticipating their safe return.

The island across the bay house on Scow Creek had a shortcut called *The Snake*. It's a natural tidal creek that winds in serpentine fashion through the center of the island making the transit from the northeast side of the bay faster when the tide is high. As the boys approached through The Snake, Peachy and Jack stared from within the bay house at the unbelievable site.

Partially covered by the marsh, it appeared to them as if a creature sprouting eight-foot-tall bulrush grass from its back weaved its way across the island. As it exited on the far side of the channel and turned toward the bay house, the boys' laughter rang out from inside the insanely decorated *Jelly Boat*.

They had harvested not only thatch, but also about a hundred *Phragmites* (frag-MITE-ease) reeds and fastened them vertically to the gunwales of the boat. Their tufted golden tops stood several feet above the boys' heads and swayed backward in the wind making it look like a miniature motorized island.

Not long after, the *Jelly Boat* suffered the fate of many old wooden vessels. It listed in the crick, tied behind the bay house, akin to a horse being put out to pasture. It rose and fell with the tides and only moved when blocking another boat or bay house project. But its days of being useful hadn't quite ended.

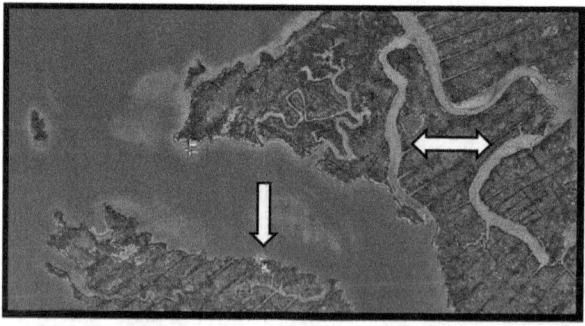

Aerial view of Scow Creek showing "The Snake" (double arrow) and its proximity to the 998 Scow Creek bay house (single arrow).

Horseshoe

crabs, ancient relatives of scorpions, made great blue crab trap bait. Mike thought the *Jelly Boat* could serve as the perfect container for storing these captured creatures for future use. As many inventive ideas at the bay house go unfinished, this one proved no different.

Weeks passed and the horseshoe crabs sadly perished in the stagnant, diluted water. This went unnoticed until the three boys detected the foul odor. First, John and Jeff tossed clam shells at the dead crabs. Bubbles of hydrogen sulfide, sulfur dioxide, and methane rose from inside the milky water and broke the cloudy film releasing their noxious contents into the salty air. As the two younger boys continued this mischief, Mike disappeared for several minutes, only to return with Uncle Mush's loaded 12-gauge shotgun. They called it the *Red Ryder* because of its rusty exterior.

"Sure, Mike. That's a great idea. It'll be like shootin' fish in a barrel," is what the boys didn't say. Instead, they stood in speechless awe at the possibilities soon to be revealed. Their lack of verbal encouragement only served to bolster their older partner-in-crime's intentions.

"Watch this, guys." Mike's infamous cue line for disaster.

John and Jeff covered their ears.

Mike aimed the aged firearm at the center of the seething mass of death inside the *Jelly Boat's* rotten hold and pulled the oxidized trigger.

BOOM!

A wave of putrid water rained down upon the boys. But that paled in comparison to the eyeball-sized chunk of decomposed horseshoe crab flesh that landed on Mike's right cheek with a SPLAT. He dropped the gun onto the dock and bolted for the bay house.

John and Jeff screamed and followed closely behind. When they reached the door, a puddle of Mike's regurgitated lunch greeted them.

"Get . . . in the water," Mike yelled from within the house's dark interior.

The boys heeded and jumped from the deck, onto the marsh, then into the chest-deep crick. They splashed water over their faces and hair.

Mike exited, ran down the dock, and leapt over the railing

straight into the water. A stream of vomit left his mouth in midair before he splashed down. He produced a bar of bath soap, lathered up his face and hair, then passed it to the boys.

White suds grew around them as the ebbing tide carried the stench of their misdeed toward the Atlantic Ocean.

What happened to the *Jelly Boat* remains a mystery to this day. It may very well have washed away in a hurricane or nor'easter. If any boat could have a soul, perhaps it haunts the back cricks of the marshes to this day. But to the last, its existence entertained, sustained, and enlightened all who experienced it.

The author, c. 1982, holding a horseshoe crab harvested for crab trap bait.

II

They all come, and they all leave. Sometimes it's a week. Sometimes just overnight. But more often only for a few hours. Through each visit, my walls, although altered several times over the years, ravaged by storms and reincarnated afterward, have never failed to protect the inhabitants during their stays.

After all, their hands built me years ago and still maintain me today. Sure, occasionally their actions scratch my paint, punch a hole, or crack a window. But deliberate action to reduce my integrity had never been an issue. I'm too precious a commodity to these beings. Anyone can buy a house on the mainland. No one can buy a bay house.

To an outsider, one who never experienced the sunsets and sunrises from my windows or listened to the haunting harmonies of the *hawk* as it broke upon the siding, or the lapping of waves on my pilings during spring tides, I would appear as nothing more than an abandoned shack. A ramshackle cottage in need of a painting, electricity, and running water. A mere hermitage.

Little did they know, as they passed by in their expensive yachts or fifty-foot fishing party boats destined to remain in the confines of the narrowly placed red and green navigational beacons, that just inside my door a comfortable set of well-used couches and armchairs awaited those who had the means to cross the shallow sandbar. The enigma of my existence must gnaw at them as they go about their travels.

Twelve could sleep soundly in beds on my first and second

floor. A fully stocked kitchen, laden with proper cooking implements, canned goods, fresh water, and condiments stood at the ready to nourish whoever needed them. And a supply of firewood always stood in a neatly arranged stack against the eastern wall. Fishing poles, tools, books and magazines, a first-aid kit, and even a few bottles of liquor kept anyone who visited satisfied. One could refer to me as a *bed and breakfast on the bay*.

My hospitality had only been taken advantage of once or twice when brigands, modern-day pirates, broke in and abused my amenities. Minor disturbances to my existence, considering a few of my unlucky counterparts on other islands around the bay had been set ablaze, diminished within an hour to a pile of wet ash only to be absorbed back into the ecosystem as fertilizer for seagrass and algae on the next high tide.

Thankfully, most who needed me returned to the mainland after their visit only to leave my insides in good order. Once, a total stranger to my conveniences happened upon me in foul weather. My caretakers would never have known of his coming and going if not for the neatly written note left behind on the dining room table.

Dear Bay Shack Owners,

I sure was lucky to come across your little house here in my hour of need. You see, a terrible storm met me while traveling from Jones Beach Inlet back to my home in Oceanside. If it hadn't been for your shack appearing out of nowhere, I would certainly have hit a sandbar or been struck by lightning. Don't worry. I put out the fire and cleaned my dish. Sorry about the glass pane in the door. I had to get inside somehow. Here's $20 to replace it.

Thank you.

The man never left his name, and we never heard from him again. But it's experiences such as this that give me hope for the future. Hope for my continued need and for an extension of kindness and respect toward people.

One

The three boys always found ways to escape their regular duties as students, sons, and stable members of society. They were good at heart and only desired what all teenagers wanted: freedom from responsibility, a degree of independence, and an occasional escape from reality.

Mike had already taken his unannounced leave the year before by running away from home and disappearing for a week. Now, the younger boys wanted a turn to revolt in like style.

After being caught for skipping school in 9th grade, John and Jeff decided running away to the bay house would be better than going home to face the inevitable wrath of their parents. The only things they considered were how to get there and what they could eat. Food and freedom to do what they wanted. What more could teenage boys care about?

These are the things they should have considered: the unforgiving cold of January in New York, a boat outside the bay house would certainly give away their location, and all the food and water would be frozen, even the cans. Hunting season had ended weeks ago. Was there even enough firewood to sustain them?

Mike provided the plan. After all, he was the expert on running away for minor reasons. He went to a friend's house and grabbed a package of freezer-burnt hot dogs. They loaded into his garvey and headed out across the frigid bay. They took with them no extra clothes, no other food or water, and no strategy for when or how they'd return.

When Mike dropped them off that afternoon, they planned for him to return the next day and bring more food.

They boys boiled ice on the potbelly stove for fresh water. There were still several stacks of canned goods left from last fall's hunting trips, as long as they could be defrosted safely. And at least a half cord of cut firewood lay neatly piled outside. They could have lived out there in comfort for a couple of weeks.

Boredom set in rather quickly once the necessities had been seen to. On the second day, the boys took to playing poker with a sticky overused deck of cards. They kept the fire burning at a vigorous pace to keep the biting cold at bay. The only warmth could be found sitting directly around the stove. They shifted the tattered furniture ever closer as the hours drifted by. The temperature steadily dropped as one walked farther from the fire until the point that if a glass of water sat upon the windowsill only ten feet away, it would freeze overnight in the uninsulated house.

The third day proved a challenge to keeping their minds occupied. What had they thought would end this reckless adventure? The temperature had dropped so greatly, that using the outhouse could cause frostbite. Finally, John just had to go. He gave it a good try, but the cold overpowered any attempts at relief. He grabbed a bushel basket on his way back inside and lined it with a plastic garbage bag. His makeshift deposit station stood right in the middle of the kitchen floor. The smell that followed doesn't need explanation here. And opening the windows for fresh air would have caused hypothermia.

Jeff frantically searched through the various cabinets for some relief while holding his nose. He eventually found a container of baby powder and a bottle of dime store perfume left by a visitor last summer. The older men had jokingly referred to the fragrance as *fifi juice*. It smelled of watered-down tobacco blended with citrus.

He threw a handful of powder at John in retribution for his odious act.

John returned the attack with a spray of the perfume.

This continued until the bay house took on an air never meant to accompany its rustic, masculine interior.

The sun had just set, and the boys settled down to a game of poker. Glasses of iced tea made from a powdered mix, blended with Smirnoff vodka they found in an old, open bottle, sat barely touched on the Formica table. Wood burned fiercely inside the rotund firebox and the subsequent smoke pouring from the chimney served as a telltale sign for searching eyes.

A mile away on the mainland, Jeff Sr. scanned the horizon with binoculars from the shoreline in South Freeport. Mush had informed him that smoke could been seen at the bay house, but no boat was docked out front. Most boats at this time of year had been pulled from the water to protect them from the crushing force of ice.

Jeff Sr.'s breath fogged the binocular's lenses. "Whoever's there didn't raise the flag." Flying Old Glory meant the house was occupied and visitors welcomed. All signs pointed to the boys' location. He got in his car and drove to Jack's house.

An hour later, not long after sunset, the red and green bow lights of a small vessel appeared as it rounded the bend from Baldwin Bay into Scow Creek.

Jeff jumped out of his chair. "Quick, turn off the lantern."

"It's too late." John stood. "They already know we're here."

Both boys prepared emotionally for what they knew was about to happen.

The hum of the outboard engine ceased as the boat stopped at the floating dock. Heavy steps vibrated the house as two men stomped on the deck through the darkness.

Jack nearly tore the door off its hinges upon entering. Jeff Sr. entered after.

The boys' fathers scanned the interior. Playboy magazine centerfolds hung on one wall, poker chips sat in uneven piles on the table, and dirty clothes hung on the backs of chairs.

Jack slammed the door and immediately opened it again after taking a few breaths of the air inside. His stern voice made the boys tremble. "How long did you two think you could live out here like Huckleberry Finn?"

Jeff Sr.'s stoicism echoed Jack's sentiments.

Jack ripped one of the centerfolds from the wall. "Get your s*** together. Let's go."

No one said another word the entire boat trip back home. Through the silence, the boys felt the damage they had done to their fathers that only a parent can feel when their child goes missing. The only consolation their parents had was that Mike knew the boys' location the whole time. He had promised them they were together and safe. Had he not relayed that information from the start, they'd probably have been in a lot more trouble and suffered a greater punishment than the grounding they received.

Even the dads knew that if their boys were to run away to anywhere, the bay house was the safest of locations for those with the desire to disappear from life for a while.

Two

Up the Crick without a Cellphone

*T*hey started as the Fresh Air Gunnin' Club. And by the time the boys had grown old enough to join as official members, the National Rifle Association-endorsed competitive shooting group had evolved and changed its name to the Scow Creek Gunnin' Club with about twenty-five members. The club met monthly throughout the year at different member's homes and six times for shotgun trap shoots at the bay house from April to September.

The bay house had a fixed ramp extending from the back deck down to the marsh and connecting to a low narrow boardwalk. The boardwalk turned right to a five-station shooting platform. The stations were about ten feet from each other. The boardwalk also veered left, over a short section that bridged a small natural crick, then ended at a *throw house* where a *puller* launched clay pigeons into the air for the shooters to try and hit.

Richie Laudman and Charlie Watson partake in a trap shoot behind the bay house, c. 1976.

John and Jeff, now young men, had enjoyed a day at a shoot

and started their way back across the bay toward the mainland after everyone had departed. John's wife, Jill, accompanied them, while Jeff's new wife, Andria, waited at home after a long day of work.

The sun had sunk low, and the chill of the evening air over the open water forced the passengers in the garvey to button up their jackets. As they navigated the first turn north toward the mainland, John's outboard motor conked out. The boat coasted to a halt and quickly succumbed to the will of the wind and tide, both counter to their desired direction of travel. They drifted toward a flooded stand of marsh and held on to the spiky grass while assessing the situation.

John tried in vain to start the engine while the sun set behind a distant Manhattan skyline. They decided it would be easier to oar their way back to the bay house and pull along the protected marsh bank than to fight the forces of nature in the waxing darkness.

After arriving a half hour later back at the bay house, they made themselves comfortable by lighting a fire and brainstorming ideas.

Jeff's beeper vibrated. Andria's phone number flashed on the narrow LCD screen. A wave of anxiety passed through his chest. He had no way of contacting her. No way to tell her he was okay and to send someone to rescue them.

John pulled out Mush's old Red Ryder shotgun, miraculously still functional. All hunters are taught that firing three shots in rapid succession into the air is a well-known distress signal. He and Jeff took turns firing off nearly an entire box of shotgun shells. Still, no boats came to their rescue. Oddly, not one boat traveled down the marked channel the entire time they were there.

The author and his wife, Andria Keene, at 998 Scow Creek, c. 1995.

Jeff's beeper

buzzed again and again throughout the evening. Eventually, the numbers '911' followed behind Andria's number. Jeff's frustration grew. He willed for Andria to put it together that they weren't just out partying and failed to update her.

The three castaways discussed sleeping arrangements as they started to accept the inevitable. They would stay stranded until someone from the mainland realized they hadn't returned.

Midnight arrived. Jeff used the bay house binoculars one last time before going to sleep in hopes for a vision of navigation lights approaching from the mainland.

Nothing.

They settled in for the night.

Two hours later, the familiar buzz of an engine resonated through the cool dense air. They leapt from their beds just in time to see Jack's boat pulling up to the floating dock. They rushed outside and welcomed him with an immediate explanation.

He told them how relieved he had been. "Andria called me an hour ago and said Jeff hadn't come home yet."

"She waited that long?" Jeff couldn't believe it.

Later he found she didn't want to assume anything and gave him the benefit of the doubt. At first, she thought they had decided to stay longer of their own free will. But after midnight, that trust turned to concern.

She called Jack and asked if she could join him.

"No. I don't know what I'm going to find out there."

If she hadn't been frightened already, that statement certainly ensued panic.

The bay house had, once again, offered a haven for the unfortunate traveler in their time of need.

Three

UP TO YOUR NECK

*M*ud. Stinky, sucking, staining mud. Many people who venture out to the bay never return for this reason only. It's everywhere. It's similar to why some people dislike the beach because of the sand or don't enjoy Domino's pizza because of the cornmeal on the crust.

Mud is a part of life in the bay. The plants absorb nutrients from it, the invertebrates live in it, and birds find food in it. People learned how to build sturdy homesteads on its slippery, sinky surface. It's land, but at the same time it's not. The marshes are mud held together by miles of plant roots.

What do teenage boys do when there's no concrete on which to bounce a basketball, no ice to shoot a hockey puck, or dirt to kick a soccer ball? They create new games! When younger, the boys made up a mud tossing activity which they coined *eguardo fights*. Imagine a *dirt bomb* or dirt clod, but instead a chunk of marsh mud the size of a softball thrown at teams hiding inside mosquito ditches exposed by the tide. Hours of fun. And when the tide rose and covered the seemingly endless supply of dark brown spongy weaponry, it was time for a cleansing swim.

Another game, famous in a small circle of south shore community teens who knew the bay boys, sprouted from a popular mainland sport but was adapted for the mushy landscape. *Marsh lacrosse* was played much like its parent game. The main difference being, well, the mud.

The boys played with one net at the end of the field and a single stick, or *take-back pole*, at the other. Whether they scored or not, the boys never left the field feeling angry or defeated. It was too much fun.

Occasionally, someone would get hurt. Mussel and razor clam shells littered the marsh. The wounds weren't usually life-threatening. A scraped knee here, a bruised shin there. But once, a friend of Mike's joined in for the first time. The boys had gotten quite rambunctious and a *king-of-the-marsh* fight started. This entailed pushing each other from the bank into the water until one was left standing triumphant. One thing led to another and during the foray he sliced his forearm open from elbow to wrist on a shell.

Cousin Jeff hurried to the bay house to grab the first-aid kit while John and Mike wrapped his arm in a T-shirt. After Jeff applied a rudimentary field dressing, Mike raced his friend by boat four miles away to the emergency room in Long Beach, the only facility accessible by boat.

Typically, mud is tolerated. But only a fool would ignore its dangers. And local bayman Jeff Korn was no fool. Korn made his living from fishing, clamming, and crabbing year-round in the bay. Even with his experience, he nearly lost his life in the mud while duck hunting with his dog Rollie in Pine Creek about a mile and a half from the bay house. Other than drowning and boating accidents, getting stuck in the mud is probably the most hazardous thing that can happen to anybody in this unique wilderness.

The boys playing marsh lacrosse.
Top: Mike and his little brother James.
Bottom: Brian O'Hare and the author.

Korn had just shot a duck from his boat. The bird plummeted through the air until it landed in the tall grass across a natural tidal creek spanning about a hundred feet. Every good hunter knows they must do everything possible to retrieve their game. The tide was low so he stepped from his boat into the mud to traverse the expanse. His boots settled down with a SQUISH. With every step they sunk deeper into the cold unforgiving mire until he could no longer move his legs.

Rollie also had trouble. His fur had become caked with the sticky muck. He barked non-stop with panic when he sensed Korn's concern.

Korn had now sunk to his waist and the tide started to rise. After many attempts, his desperation grew when the water reached his chest. With a final expenditure of energy, he wrenched his legs from the deathtrap and doggie-paddled to the boat.

Hypothermia and exhaustion had taken hold, and the only cure was warmth and fluids. The bay house held both of those needs, so he made a beeline for its welcoming walls. If it hadn't been for that haven, Korn might have become a casualty.

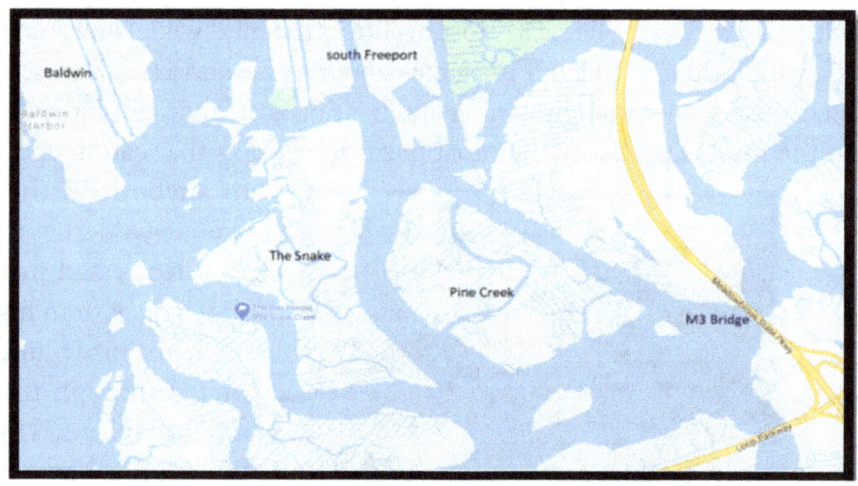

Map showing the location of the bay house and Pine Creek,
where Korn nearly perished.

III

As you've read, the bay can be a dangerous place to visit. It allowed the city folk to come as close as they could to a life in the wilderness without going hours north to the mountains or miles offshore into the deep sea.

Severe weather will blind experienced boaters as thick fog rolls in or squall lines sweep over the trackless meadows in soaking sheets. You'll not find protection from lightning or hailstorms. There are holes large enough to swallow a Mini Cooper and mud deep enough to cover it. Venomous and electrifying creatures lurk under marsh banks and others lie in wait for flying prey in silky traps spun between thick reeds. While more sit patiently with razor sharp teeth and spines to split and puncture skin. Other perils include strong currents, submerged debris, and the weakened structures of boats and banisters alike.

I wonder why they ever come out here at all. The mainland is much safer. Even the ones who suffer harm return with impunity. And each time I greet them openly. If they can forgive, so can I.

The number of times I've witnessed my visitors injure them-selves or injure others are many. Fortunately, no one ever perished in their escapades. But quite a few close calls can be mentioned here.

One

The view directly west of 998 Scow Creek. Migratory birds can be seen gathering in the water.

*F*alling overboard is always a possibility, which the complacent tend to ignore to their chagrin. Taking an unexpected dip in the winter months, however, can prove fatal.

The whole crew had just spent two days hunting ducks and other migratory waterfowl and were ready to spend their last night at the bay house. The opening day trip was always exciting, and this year proved no different. A dinner of Jack's famous clam stew simmered on the propane stovetop. Tendrils of steam carried the scent from the pot into the nostrils of hungry hunters as an orange sun hung in the air just minutes from setting.

Hundreds of flocking birds broke the silence as their calls permeated the cold, late-November air. Adrenaline coursed within the men's bloodstreams. They peered through the windows and over the crick as a flock of brant, the smaller cousins of Canada geese, swooped over the water from the east. Their white bellies reflected the setting sun's rays.

Two generations of hunters leapt from their seats, scrambled for their shotguns and ammunition, and fought to be the first shooters out the door. From the deck, with bellies pressed against the banister and feet planted firmly on the planking, they unloaded their firearms into the dense flock of passing birds.

Jack's black Labrador retriever, Turk, shook with the anticipation of getting his mouth on a fallen brant. Once the hunters stopped firing, Jack held Turk's collar to prevent him from leaping from the dock.

About nine brant plummeted through the air. A single shooter probably wouldn't have fired at all because the birds had kept their distance from the bay house. Perhaps previous brushes with loud noises taught them to stay away from such structures in flight. The felled fowl splashed down halfway across the crick. The tide flowed rapidly out carrying the injured and dead birds away.

Jack let Turk go. With a bolt of energy like that of Olympic sprinters, the dog leapt from the dock, onto the marsh, and into the frigid water. He swam nearly four hundred feet from the bay house and grabbed the first bird.

Other birds, only injured, drew Turk's attention. The flapping wings on the surface of the water and guttural grunts were too tempting for him. He dropped the first and turned in the deep water for a more active and enticing target.

After doing this three times, instead of returning immediately with the first bird, concern spread across Jack's face. "John, get in the boat and get that dumb dog."

John made his way to the dock, and Jeff joined him. It would take two of them to pull the dog into the boat.

The garvey skipped across the water and covered the distance in less than a minute. All the while Turk continued to grab at several different birds, oblivious of the fact that he'd be too tired to swim all the way back to shore.

John put the engine in neutral. "Turk, come!"

The boys wrestled the dog into the boat then wiped wet black fur off their hands.

John scanned the carnage around them while he held Turk's collar. Injured brant flapped single wings to no avail. Dead birds floated, their mangled feathers breaking the reddened water. "Look at all that blood."

Jeff swung his head to see. The force loosed the glasses from his head and sent them flying over the gunwale and into the icy channel. He watched as they rapidly descended into the clear winter water. "My three-hundred-dollar glasses!"

John reached after them with lightning speed. First his fingers entered the water. Then his arm. And much like a slinky when it cascades down a staircase, his shoulder, his head, his torso, and his legs followed.

The evasive spectacles sunk to Davey Jones' locker, and John was following at a frightening speed.

Historically, the usual hunting paraphernalia involved an eclectic assemblage of coats, gloves, hats, and foul weather gear that simply needed to be drab in color. The boys never used camouflage face paint or expensive equipment from famous outdoor catalogue companies.

But footwear needed to be waterproof. And what boots were more waterproof than fireman's boots? All the men, both generations, had been volunteer firefighters. So they made good use of those pieces of turnout gear that had aged beyond their usefulness for protecting the good citizens of the Village of Freeport.

From left to right: Mike Combs (in boat), Ricky "Surf" Laudman, John Combs III, Jeff Keene II, and Brian Laudman, c. 1990.

John wore a pair of those boots. And as he fell into the depths, they filled with cold water becoming equivalent to the cement galoshes made infamous in New York City Mafia stories.

The last part of his body to leave the safety of the boat grasped the gunwale. His white knuckles told of both the force needed to defy the pull of gravity and the fear running through his mind.

Jeff sprung to the side, took hold of John's arm, and pulled with all his might.

John's drenched body poured over the side and hit the floor of the boat with a splashy thud.

After catching his breath, he met eyes with Jeff. "Sorry, man. I couldn't reach 'em in time."

Jeff plopped onto the painted plank seat spanning the center of the boat. "That's okay. My dad got them for about twenty-five dollars anyway." His dad was a licensed optician.

"What!" John shoot upright. "You said they were three-hundred dollars!"

Both boys laughed, mainly at the relief of averting disaster. They fished the remaining brant from the water and got back to the bay house to get John a change of clothes.

"What happened out there?" Jack couldn't stop laughing when he saw his soaking wet bedraggled son.

Jeff Sr. regretted leaving his camera up shore. "We saw a splash and lot of movement."

Everyone laughed and gave thanks for the fortunate ending.

Two

Bottled Behavior

The three boys had grown up together. And just like brothers, they knew exactly how to push each other's buttons. Combine their propensity for this and the unexpected environment surrounding the bay house, and you can imagine something surprising to ensue most of the time.

The bay house drew people from various groups throughout the years. The first being The Mystic Knights of the Sea. For years, a hand-painted plaque hung on the wall with various names, including that of George "Mush" Carmen and Bud Wright. Apparently, these gentlemen were the ones responsible for bringing the bay house out here and finishing its construction all those years ago. The stories of their early escapades, including the other members, that sign, and how they came upon that regal title, have been lost to history, buried in the aftermath of Hurricane Gloria since 1985. Other groups included several of the mainland's volunteer fire companies, both from Freeport and the neighboring town of Baldwin. The bay house even hosted a fire department all the way from Mahopac, a hamlet in upstate New York.

James Combs and Brian O'Hare build a makeshift fort next to a crick with a large piece of Styrofoam, c. 1986.

Finally, the Scow Creek Gunnin' Club took advantage of the unique setting every summer for their annual family picnic. More than twenty-five families gathered on the docks, decks, and around the dining room table. At times, there were so many boats they had to string them together end-to-end to save space at the dock. Several vessels even anchored off in the distance, and their passengers ferried in to join the festivities.

Barbeques churned out a cow's worth of hot dogs and hamburgers, while pots of clam stew and boiled corn-on-the-cob simmered away in the kitchen and on potbelly stove. The children enjoyed every minute. No yucky vegetables found their way across the bay to poison their plates. Bags of chips, cheese doodles, and pretzels were the only side dishes required out there. Orange soda and chocolatey Yoo-hoo flowed like water.

Frisbees and balls flew around the marsh like confetti. The younger boys constructed forts on the marsh out of spare lumber and Styrofoam. The girls sought fiddler crabs as temporary but entertaining pets. And the parents sat back and wished their kids could be this easily entertained at home. After all, none of them could afford a swimming pool. Why did they need one with this wonderful gift of nature right here?

But like many moments of well-earned serenity, where all is as it should be and everyone is having a marvelous time, the pleasure can be broken with such a force that the shock waves can be felt years later.

Mike was adept at teasing everyone, no matter the age or sex. Although John's older brother, his cousin Jeff tended to react with more vigor in response to the incessant taunting.

The older boys played catch with a football behind the bay house while the younger children kept busy on the perimeter. At one point, the ball flew over John and Jeff's heads and landed in the narrow mosquito ditch behind them.

Mike ran to get the ball.

Jeff got there first.

Mike, far stronger, lifted Jeff up from behind and squeezed.

Jeff hollered and dropped the football in the marsh.

Mike didn't let go.

Jeff squirmed and tried in vain to escape Mike's crushing bearhug.

Finally, Mike let go, picked up the ball, and ran to his end of the playing field.

Jeff's anger rose uncontrollably. He wanted to lash out at Mike for hurting and embarrassing him in front of the other children. He scanned the marsh below his sneakered feet for anything to help vent his rage.

An old brown beer bottle, half full of saltwater and sulfurous mud, presented itself through thin strands of marsh grass.

Jeff reached down without thinking, took hold, and blindly threw it into the air.

The bottle spun end-over-end through the blue sky. It never came close to Mike. Instead, as fate dictated, it struck a galvanized cleat on the bow of a garvey that had been docked against the bank of the crick behind the bay house. The brown bottle shattered into numerous razor-sharp shards.

Standing on the bow of that boat was a young boy named Timmy. Timmy wasn't wearing any shoes. A piece sliced its way across the top of his foot. The screams that followed stopped everyone in their tracks.

Jeff ran up to the boat. He froze in terror at the site of blood spreading over the wet bow beneath Timmy's feet.

One of the adults ran over and swept Timmy into his arms. Everyone panicked, especially the parents, because none of them knew if the screaming was coming from their own child or not. And no one knew how the accident occurred in the first place.

Only Jeff knew exactly how it happened.

He meandered in shock through the growing crowd of onlookers as he made his way to where he last saw his parents.

His mother found him, half expecting him to be the wounded one. "What happened?" She looked him up and down for injuries.

"I . . . hurt Timmy."

"What? What do you mean? How?"

"I got mad at Michael and threw a bottle. It cut his foot . . . bad."

His mother's anger soon abated when worry over what her son

had done to another child surpassed it. She escorted Jeff to a family member's sailboat and made him stay there until ready to leave.

A few days went by. Jeff's parents made him visit Timmy after he'd been patched up. He brought a Lego set as an apology.

No permanent damage had been done. And Jeff and Mike both learned valuable lessons that day.

Three

A Bloodsucker got Him!

*C*lamming in front of the bay house had its rewards as well as its perils. Primarily, shellfishing closures imposed by local agencies due to rain, season, or site rotations controlled the drive to search for the hard-shelled delicious creatures. But the clam's uses proved too great to abide by the rules enforced by bay constables. Besides, it was usually just the kids who ventured out in front of the bay house for a half bushel or so when the tide ebbed.

The author, center, and his cousins, Mike Combs on the left and John Combs III on the right.

The boys donned last year's worn-out school sneakers and traipsed through the mud. Only a fool would dare walk in the bay without some sort of foot protection. As they walked, the hard clams could be felt beneath their feet under the substrate. Reaching down into the darkness barehanded was a brave feat, and delicate precision was needed to avoid injury. Once that clam was grasped firmly in their fist, it was destined to become part of a healthy meal.

Jeff "Peachy" Keene Sr. poses with his bagged snow goose, a rare sight during hunting season at 998 Scow Creek, c. 1983.

Everyone loved Jack's homemade clam stew. The smell of spices and boiled potatoes with a hint of clam meat simmering on the propane kitchen stove could be detected the moment a visitor's boat touched the dock. Steamed quahogs on the half shell popped open on the barbeque grill while clam fritters sizzled in the pan next to the stew. People would spend a lot of money for these ultra-fresh delicacies in a Manhattan restaurant. They enjoyed them frequently at the bay house. Add in fresh eel, with muscles still twitching when chunks of the serpentine flesh were rolled in batter, flounder filets, and snow goose meat and they ate like the monarchs of old.

Ribbed mussels lined the marsh banks in bunches, held fast to the mud with strong biologically produced threads, much like a spider's. Ironically, these mollusks proved poor eating, but served as terrific bait for killifish traps. Ripping them from their holdfasts over time produced *mussel muscles* in the wrists and forearms.

Other pastimes during the receding tide, when the banks stood exposed to the air and creatures often protected by the depths lay bare, proved the most entertaining. One of those activities was hunting for fiddler crabs. These served as the most versatile and hardy pets a kid could have out in the bay.

Landlubber children use earthworms and cicadas to frighten

their friends. Not in the bay. Fiddler crabs served to terrorize both children and adults alike. Mike once let a handful of the pinching critters free in Mush's boxer drawers while he slept on a picnic bench on the deck. You can imagine his confusion and anger upon waking to that.

And that's what Jeff and his younger cousin Jimmy spent the afternoon doing that summer day. While most guests spent time lounging around the bay house, the boys hunted fiddler crabs, also good bait for fishing, and mussels along the marsh's edge a hundred feet east of the dock.

Fiddler crabs are odd looking creatures. The males wave around a gargantuan claw—often as long as their bodies—to attract females and defend their territories. But don't let its size fool you into thinking they're sluggish. When reaching for one, they zip away, disappearing into a hole. Patience and persistence were needed. But the rewards great.

Jeff caught one off guard and thrust his hand towards it. The crab fell into a larger hole and Jeff's hand followed. When he retracted his appendage, a three-inch long slice on the knuckle of his index finger issued blood.

Jimmy's jaw dropped open in terror. "A bloodsucker got you!"

All the color drained from Jeff's face as he realized a mussel shell or other keen-edged denizen of the mud had done this.

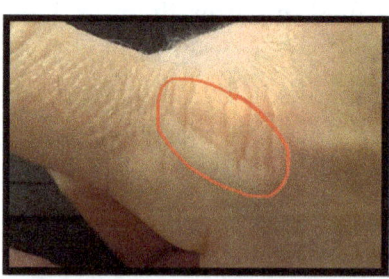

The author's hand today, still bearing the 'bloodsucker' scar.

Jimmy ran screaming, "A bloodsucker got him! A bloodsucker got him!" He scrambled up the bank and bolted to the bay house for help. Even though the carnivorous, venomous bloodworms do live in the mud, one could never produce a wound this bad. Jimmy hadn't processed this information.

Jeff followed behind holding his arm up as crimson drops sprinkled onto the green marsh grass.

Thankfully, an important and rare visitor to the bayhouse that day was Jimmy's grandmother, Martha Combs. Being a retired nurse, she knew just what to do. "No stitches. I'll just clean it, and you'll be good as new."

Jeff still bears the scar forty years later and every time he sees it, he thinks of that day and the adventures they all had, both good and bad. People never look back and recall their best day watching television or playing video games. But a single day on the bay can produce memories for a lifetime.

Clam Stew

~John "Jack" E. Combs Jr.

It may not look complicated, but that's the beauty of its design. Jack was famous for his clam stew, and you could detect the boiling pot's tangy scent long before you entered the bay house. Just never call it "clam soup" or "clam chowder." And using fresh clams is a must. Avoid canned meat at all costs, as this meal is best prepared with those mollusks you dig up yourself.

Ingredients

- 3 or 4 dozen chowder clams
- 4 lbs. potatoes, diced
- 1 ½ lbs. onions, sliced
- ¼ lb. salt pork
- 1 tablespoon thyme

Directions

1. Brown salt pork, then set aside. Be sure to save ½ the grease.
2. Cook potatoes and onions with the juice from the clams. Be sure potatoes and onions are covered with clam juice. If not, add water.
3. Mix in salt pork, saved grease, and thyme.
4. Let cook until potatoes are done.
5. Add chopped clams and cook for 10–15 minutes.
6. Shut off heat and let sit for ½ hour before serving.

Fried Eel

*M*any would call eel an exotic food. And most would shy away from it here in the States. But eel has been enjoyed on Long Island and its surrounding waters since long before European settlers arrived. Although Native Americans typically smoked eel meat, frying them is a lot faster, and you'll swear by the taste. After all, an eel is just a long, skinny fish. And the fresher, the better. It makes a great appetizer or even a main course. It's like fish and chips meets popcorn chicken!

Ingredients

- 2 lbs. fresh eel, cleaned (head and innards removed) and skinned (about 2 eels)
- 1 cup all-purpose flour
- 2 eggs, beaten
- Salt and white pepper to taste
- Vegetable oil for frying
- Lemon wedges for serving

Directions

1. Rinse the cleaned, skinned eel under cold water and pat it dry with paper towels. Cut the eel into manageable pieces, about 2–3 inches long.
2. Soak the eel in salted water for about 20 minutes.
3. Season the pieces with salt and white pepper according to taste.

4. Place the flour in a shallow dish. Dredge each piece of eel in the flour, making sure to coat it evenly on all sides. Shake off any excess.

5. Dip each floured eel piece into the beaten eggs, ensuring they are well coated.

6. Heat vegetable oil in a deep frying pan over medium-high heat. Once the oil is hot (around 350°F or 180°C), carefully place the eel pieces into the oil, a few at a time, making sure not to overcrowd the pan. Fry the eel for about 3–4 minutes on each side, or until they are golden brown and crispy.

7. Once fried, remove the eel pieces from the oil using a slotted spoon or tongs and transfer them to a plate lined with paper towels to drain any excess oil.

8. Serve hot, with lemon wedges on the side for squeezing over the eel for added flavor.

Four

BRO-ACTIVE

*M*ike and John spent more time in the bay than any of the other family children. As such, their brushes with disaster numbered greater than average. Of all the known stories involving only these brothers, two tales tie for the blue ribbon.

Bay house parties were exceptional events. Where else could you gather fifty people, make as much ruckus as you want, as late as you want, without disturbing neighbors, and at the same time be deep in nature? Yes, you needed a boat to get there. Yes, you had to use an outhouse when you felt the urge. And cellphones? Practically science fiction in the late 1970s.

This particular celebration happened to fall upon Independence Day, right between both boys' early July birthdays. Dock space was limited, so boats had been tied in long chains of interconnected bow lines stretching east and kept taught by the outgoing tide.

A favorite summer diversion was towing someone at the back of a boat. Formally, this activity includes waterskiing, tubing, and the like. But in the bay, the boys made do with what they had. And boat cushions made for suitable replacements—light, cheap, and soft.

The boys were young. John around eight and Mike two years older. It was John's first time alone at the tiller and his turn to pull Mike back and forth in front of the bay house.

"Just keep it straight," Mike explained to his inexperienced brother before leaping with glee over the side into the turbid chilly water.

The boat's eight-horsepower outboard didn't provide enough power to be overly dangerous, but there's one thing to understand when considering an engine operated by the Combs boys. There were only two speeds: stop and full throttle. These settings are voluntary, of course, but the practice held firm on this day.

All seemed well on the first run as John captained the vessel and towed his brother behind him. Then, Mike let go of his float. Not challenged by swimming nor depth of water, only the cessation of continued thrills, he called out to his brother. "Hey! Come back and get me!"

Happy to oblige, John pushed the tiller to starboard and the small wood boat cut through the water as it turned and headed toward Mike. John shouted back, "I'm coming to pick you up!"

The boat's little motor couldn't quite make the vessel plane off, so the bow rode high out of the water blocking John's view of anything directly in front. That included Mike.

Mike's eyes widened as his brother drove right at him. There was no getting out the way. Instead, he dipped under the surface and pushed himself backward through the water all the way down until his back lay flat on the seaweed-covered bottom.

The boat passed right over him with its spinning propeller churning the water just inches above his face.

Life's instructions often come at you fast and with unexpected consequences. And no faster than a brush with death when you've not even hit puberty yet. So, when John took the tiller a second time, a new opportunity for learning presented itself.

On another day, the boys again took turns pulling each other behind their garvey. John was at the tiller. This time, when he turned around to

*Mike and his cousin
Elizabeth "Betty Jean" (Keene) Engel, c. 1978.*

pick up his brother, the towline caught him by the neck and pushed him over the side and into the water. What was the lesson for this round of play? Tie the rope to the stern rather than the bow.

Mike's jaw dropped as his boat continued its full-speed unmanned journey toward the bay house. He and John yelled for help and everyone on the dock drew their attention to the commotion out on the water. They moved to assist. But it was too late.

The runaway vessel was sure to collide with the boats stretched out in its path. It missed the first one and turned by itself to weave through the whole line of boats without striking any of them. It ultimately rammed into the marsh right behind the floating dock without hitting anyone or anything. Talk about blind luck.

The events allowing one's life to pass before their eyes are numerous in the bay. Countless experiences like the ones above reflect those times when you realize God must have a further purpose for your existence, even if it's just to have others read about it and laugh.

Five

A common site on the marsh behind 998 Scow Creek was a competitive trap shoot.
Seen shooting here is Jack Combs, c. 1991.

Numerous tumbles occurred over the years, most harmless but all part of life on the bay. Boats are rocky, decks are slippery, and railings, over time, become rickety. Harsh weather and sub-par materials, such as flotsam planks and re-used fasteners, held up far less longer than those bought new from the hardware store. John Combs Sr. had the habit of hammering out old nails, bending them straight, and using them again. He called them *D'Agostinos*. Today, his grandsons have no idea why.

Gun club competitive trap shoots often brought visitors who wouldn't otherwise venture out to the bay house. They either didn't own a boat or were too far removed from life on the bay to spend any more than a couple of hours a month there. Perhaps it was the rustic feel of splintered wood on their buttocks when using the outhouse or the jumbo house spiders, made fat by gorging on swarms of green flies and gnats, festooning the windows. In any case, when push came to shove, their extra weight made a difference on the bay house's structural integrity. Railings often gave way but never at more unfortunate times than when a male guest relieved himself over the edge into the marsh below.

A competitive shoot had just ended, and hamburgers sizzled on the propane barbeque. As the attendees lounged about, now only shooting the breeze and anticipating lunch, the entire deck gave way directly under the grill. One member, John Stuerzel, took the brunt of gravity's dangerous pull.

They all expected him to be impaled by a rusty pipe or sliced open from stem to stern by an errant D'Agostino. Venturing beneath the bay house under normal conditions was dangerous enough. But falling into it through a rotten hole in the decking was another situation all together.

Miraculously, Stuerzel stood up in the mud and found himself sporting nothing more than a few scrapes and a torn pair of shorts. They helped him out of the void and immediately gathered the troops to rebuild the missing deck from the supply of collected marsh wood on the rack behind the bay house.

Peachy once scored a perfect landing after falling, as they say, 'ass over tea kettle' into the water from the bow of the boat when trying

The trap shooting range behind the Seaman bay house on Big Crow Island in East Bay.

to secure it to the floating dock. His accomplishment had been entirely judged upon the fact that he flipped over headfirst into the water with a lit cigarette in his mouth, all while being three sheets to the wind.

When he righted him-self, after his feet found the muddy bottom, with that smoking cigarette still clinging haphazardly to his lower lip, the entire company at the bay house erupted in laughter.

Another story tells of Mike climbing down to his boat using a rusted metal ladder. He held a Cole-man lantern in one hand and wore a raccoon hat. The rungs broke under his weight, and he plummeted into the cold water up to his neck.

Mike Combs and the author exact repairs after the deck collapsed.

He looked up at his friend Steve Trimboli, the tail of his coon skin cap dripping wet, and said, "At least I saved the lantern."

Six

SHARK TALES

$\mathcal{M}$ike had always been one for trying to scare his younger family members into believing something true when the opposite had always been the case. It didn't matter where they were, he needed to frighten them into thinking a structural malfunction or dangerous creature was about to end their lives. Rocking a Ferris wheel's gondola while yelling, "There's a loose bolt," and jumping up and down in an ascending elevator were two of his classic taunts.

Once, he terrorized Ricky "Surf" Laudman when he overtwisted the head from a duck while attempting to quickly dispatch it and reduce its suffering after it had been shot. Its head popped right off. The duck's body stumbled around the floor of the boat shooting blood everywhere while Surf screamed and recoiled almost to the point of falling overboard. Situations out in the bay were perfect for this type of psychological torture, intentionally caused or otherwise.

Mike, John, Jeff, and their close friend Surf decided to go clamming in the crick just west of the bay house. After about an hour, the hawk picked up, and the

An aerial view of 998 Scow Creek.

tide began to rise. Conditions for clamming took a dive, so the boys decided to head back.

Trudging through the waist-deep water proved a challenge. Why not break up the monotony with a good ol' panic?

Mike's eyes widened. "Guys, I think a shark just brushed pass my leg."

An argument ensued amongst the boys about the possibility of sharks large enough to eat someone being found in Scow Creek.

Surf took the bait and lost his nerve. He strode with haste through the choppy, deepening water, unable to see or feel his footfalls. While the other boys laughed at his distress, he stepped on something sharp and cut open his foot.

The distance between Surf and the boys grew until they saw him disappear into the bay house alone. By the time they caught up and entered the doorway, a disturbing site met them.

Surf sat at the table in the main room slumped over a yellow plastic bowl containing vomit. He held a ball of blood-spotted paper towels to his wounded foot.

Mike sat next to him while John and Jeff stood nearby. He leaned toward Surf. "You gonna be okay?"

Unsteadily, he replied through pale lips. "I'm all right, guys."

In the confusion, the screen door had been left open and a greenfly entered uninvited. These biting creatures will draw blood and, along with swarms of gnats, are the scourge of the bay. The wind usually keeps them away. But this one couldn't resist access to warm-bodied creatures in a windless enclosure. Perhaps it was the scent of blood that drew it near.

Jeff saw it first. "Surf, there's a big greenfly on your leg."

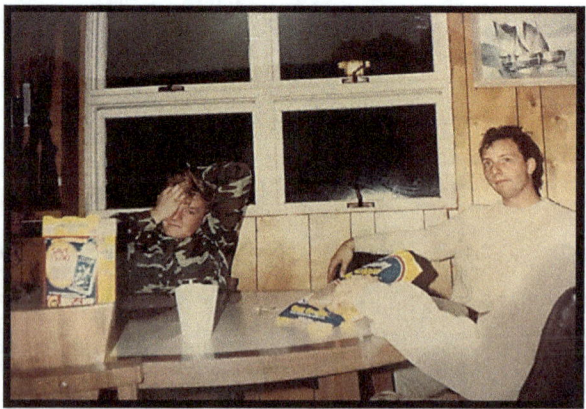

Ricky "Surf" Laudman and John E. Combs III during a hunting trip at 998 Scow Creek, c. 1995.

Surf's next act may not amaze you, but it's unheard of to those who've swatted these parasites on a frequent basis. They're fast and often missed when aiming and swinging hard. This was something right out of *The Karate Kid* when Daniel Larusso catches a fly with his chopsticks and Mr. Miyagi says in broken English, "You beginner luck."

Surf nonchalantly moved his hand to his thigh, hovering over the fly. His hand dropped onto it. He picked the insect up between his fingers and proceeded to roll it as one would dispatch a booger. When done, he tossed it into the bowl of barf. No truer story has been told.

Seven

DOGGONE

After gun club competitions, boaters often traveled in pairs to insure a safe return to the mainland. On this day, Jimmy boated alongside his father, Jack, and a passenger, Jeff "J.B." Blossom. Jimmy had the family dog, Turk, onboard.

As they motored down the channel, Jimmy noticed the inebriation levels of everyone in his father's boat. He decided to give them some room. He pointed his vessel to exit the channel and drive over the flats.

His boat had been designed for a small engine, perhaps a five horsepower. But his only choice had been to put a fifteen horsepower on the transom. When he opened the throttle to plane the boat off to keep the propeller from hitting bottom, the hull of the boat fell away.

Turk disappeared under the boat.

Jimmy stopped the engine fearing the worst had happed to his black Lab. He looked over at his father's vessel to see J.B. pointing and throwing up his arms.

Afterwards, Jimmy learned that J.B. had been telling Jack, "I think your son's going down!"

Jack replied, "No, no. He's okay."

"I don't know, Jack. I think he's going down."

Jack finally turned the boat and came to Jimmy's rescue.

Turk had popped up far behind the engine in a mass of frothy water, miraculously missing the propeller. They saved the outboard. But the rotten boat was scuttled.

IV

Hunting & Fishing

People have hunted these shores long before I ever found my place here on the marsh. Even before I had been built on the mainland. From what I've heard, the skies would be blackened with passing flocks of migratory waterfowl numbering in the tens of thousands. They still pass, but in lesser quantities, every fall and winter. Even the number of hunters has diminished.

Looking east toward the sunrise, the guys sometimes kept their guns are the ready in case a flock flew near the bay house.

Brant arrive in large flocks, sometimes with several hundred birds. A raucous chorus of guttural *Crrrronks* signal their arrival. When they land in shallow water, they spend the night lulling hunters to sleep from a distance. Geese honk as they pass, preferring inland grassy fields over the salty marsh reeds. And ducks of all species slip into back cricks and tidal ponds to feed and rest until taking their predawn flights southward to gentler climes.

Preparing for the arrival of these wild birds starts in summer, months before hunting season. My caretakers bring cords of wood to cut. The chainsaw screams as the fuel pile grows. Just weeks before in mid-fall, boats are decked out with layers of green and gold spartina grass, as if decorating for Christmas. The green portions will brown just in time for the season to start.

Finally, they arrive. Tomorrow is opening day. In the morning, the sounds of gunfire, a dog barking, and stories of victories and failures will issue forth from elated hunters.

But the bay is the wilderness. A vast treeless expanse of perils. And the hunters toyed with these dangers, welcoming them time and again, year after year. There were many close calls and even closer realities.

One

Mush owned 998 Scow Creek. The Combs' family leased another house only 500 hundred feet east until Hurricane Gloria took it in 1985. "Uncle Mush" adopted them into his bay house, and the lease was eventually put in Jack's name.

Mush was a unique character and a man who understood how blessed bay house owners were. He is quoted as saying, "You don't hear no loud car mufflers or dogs barking all night. It's quiet."

He once won a raffle, and the prize was a Thanksgiving turkey. When he arrived to collect it, you can imagine his surprise when the butcher handed him a live Tom turkey over the meat counter.

In his gruff weathered voice, Mush asked, "What am I supposed to do with this?"

The man replied matter-of-factly, "Eat it."

He got the bird home and released it into the garage to await its fate. He went inside and downed a fifth of rye whiskey in preparation for the morbid task awaiting him.

He grabbed a baseball bat and another swig of liquid courage, then entered the garage and closed the door behind him.

998 Scow Creek prior to 1985.

Bang! Crash! The noises emanating from inside made the neighbors cringe.

Mush emerged thoroughly scratched up and exhausted with a dead turkey over his shoulder.

When he arrived at the butcher later, he flopped it down onto the counter.

The shocked butcher gawked at the beaten and bruised bird. "What did you do to this thing?"

Mush, ever blunt, answered, "It was either him . . . or me."

The exceptional man possessed a singular wit.

George "Mush" Carmen celebrating an event at Hose Co. #1, in Freeport.

Hunting season provided an audience for Mush's one-of-a-kind humor, and the boys loved every quip and wisecrack. So when one of the men brought back a duck from the morning hunt with a federal tracking band on its leg, he couldn't help himself.

Leg bands discovered on migratory waterfowl are rare finds. When discovered, a hunter had to send the band to the U.S. Fish and Wildlife Service. Nowadays, it's all reported online. This band had the letters 'IVL' stamped into its metal surface along with a series of numbers afterwards.

As they passed around the small ring, someone inquired, "I wonder what the letters mean?"

Mush's snappy retort was, "'I Vly Low.'"

His answer is a story repeated every hunting trip since and has come to define any bird easily taken without much skill.

Two

The Magic Shell Box

John Sr., whose CB radio handle had been Wild Duck, had a peculiar, old-world way about him. When one thought of the kind man, ideas of decoy carving, flannel shirts, and colorful colloquialisms came to mind. This was a man whose resourcefulness and skillset went unmatched. Afterall, he'd survived the Great Depression, two wives, and worked at Columbian Bronze in Freeport making such varied items as boat propellers and metal social security cards.

Once, his son, Jack, came home from work and saw his father in Buckley's Lot across the street on Westend Avenue working on a . . . pink duck boat?

"Pop!" He could barely hold in the laughter. "Pop, what're you doing? You can't use this color for ducks. They ain't colorblind like deer."

"Now listen, Son. It's just the primer. Had to use up some old cans. I'm gonna paint over it soon as she dries." For all we know, that's where the modern fad of pink camouflage arose!

The very next year, John Sr. put together a few more cans of old paint and discovered a brand-new color for painting a duck boat. It looked so mottled and uneven that his son, Jack, named the color *turkey turd brindle*.

His duck boat painting jobs always turned out to work well, however, because John Sr. always ended up bagging his daily limit of birds. It also helped that he carried with him a well-stocked gunnin' box.

But how do hunters learn how to hunt? From an older, more experienced hunter, of course. And every kind of hunter, be it wild boar, deer, fish, or duck, must learn what works and what will set you up for failure in each unique environment and particular target prey. And the more knowledge and experience you have, the less gear you pack.

Jack learned from his father how to hunt duck. They'd go through all the motions: waking up well before dawn, dressing in camouflaged winter gear, traveling to their secret spot, setting out decoys, and securing the boat in the marsh. And when finally settled, they could relax and wait for the birds to come.

But that gunnin' box had magic in it.

One cold morning, little Jack waited while his father fell asleep. He snuck his hand into the box to find it stocked with Social Tea cookies, a thermos of tea, and a roll of Tums antacids.

Jack took advantage of his father's unconsciousness and devoured everything, even the antacids.

Years later, in the mid-1970s, Jack recounted the story on cassette tape while sitting around the table at the bay house during an opening day trip:

"I thought they were peppermints. When I woke him up an hour later, he asks, 'What'd ya do?' He was so mad when I told him. He stopped talking, picked up the decoys, and took us home." Jack chuckled. "He was so thirsty, he couldn't even breathe."

Years later, that box still held the same supplies, but the number of shotgun shells had reduced from many to just a few. John Sr. swore he didn't need any more than that. "One shell. Two birds," he'd say referencing the legal limit of certain species like black duck or mallards. Truth be told, he was such a good shot, he *could* take down two birds with one shotgun shell.

Three

BLIZZARDS & BRANDY

*Y*ears later, Jack had become a father three times over to all boys. Mike and John had grown old enough to finally go on their first duck hunt. Accompanying them were Jeff Sr. and his son Jeff II, Rich Laudman and his son Ricky, and Tom Seaman Sr. and his son Tommy.

Opening day had passed weeks ago, and Christmas was just around the corner. The frigid air grew colder as all four families met at the bay house in the afternoon of the first day. The woodburning stove couldn't keep the whole place warm enough, so they fired up a kerosene heater as well. Everyone huddled around the two heat sources waiting to see what the weather would do.

The hawk pounded with gale force fierceness against the west wall's exterior. Out by the floating dock, windswept salt water sprayed onto the ropes and boats. Near blizzard conditions developed as snow flew sideways with the whipping breeze.

The dads decided, after much deliberation and a few snorts of booze, that leaving would be the safest option. They extinguished the fire, turned off the kerosene heater, and packed up the kids. Just traveling from the door to the boats sent the boys into a shiver. When they reached the dock, to their shock the mooring lines had several inches of ice formed over them.

Jack walked back to the bay house and returned with a hatchet. He lifted his arm and hacked at the ropes until their frozen cores severed. Everyone loaded onto the boats.

Tommy, being the youngest, had stopped talking. Frostbite and hypothermia now posed a real threat, particularly to the young boys.

Before shoving off, the men decided that motoring into the wind toward Baldwin Bay would expose them too much to the elements. Taking the Snake would be the least dangerous route.

The Snake was a serpentine natural tidal creek running from the opposite side of the marshland just to the north of the bay house that opened into Scow Creek. It was narrow, protected from the wind by tall grass, and only a quarter mile longer than across the bay.

The boys took small sips of apricot brandy for warmth during the slow trip through the shallow passage. It was their first taste of liquor.

When they reached the halfway point, they hugged the mainland shore to get out of the worst of the weather. It was a trip they'd always remember and another life lesson they'd not soon forget.

Four

Fish Stories

*H*unting isn't just about birds. Deer once passed through these marshes traveling from the mainland to the barrier beaches. In one tale, John Sr. almost lost his life to a frightened buck.

Chilly winter air cut through his woolen overcoat. He'd heard rumor of large flocks of geese and rare breeds of duck gathering in the open waters where South Oyster Bay meets The Great South Bay. The trip from Freeport was about fifteen miles as the crow flies. In his dory, a boat with pointed ends and high flaring sides, it would take a couple of hours to travel that distance.

As he neared his destination, through the morning mist the visage of a large dog swam toward him. The approaching creature turned out to be a buck whitetail deer. It must have lost its way between marsh islands. Its wide eyes hinted at the fear it must have felt as it attempted to board John's small boat from the bow.

He moved forward and tried to push the panicking animal away before it capsized him. He grabbed its antlers and shoved only for it to swim right back.

The deer grunted in horror at the real threat of drowning as it lifted its front legs and threw them over the gunwale time and again.

And each time, John pushed the crazed animal off. He tried to get back to the engine to put distance between him and the buck. But with every chance he got, the deer attempted to board again.

Finally, John decided if he didn't take drastic action, he'd die in the frigid water with this deer. He couldn't use his shotgun because he didn't have a deer permit. He scanned the boat's interior for anything to help. He grabbed the oar.

He bonked the deer right between the antlers.

After a few blows, the deer got the idea that this was not the best tactic for survival and swam off back into the mist and out of sight.

John plopped down onto his seat at the tiller to catch his breath. He then decided he'd had enough excitement for one day and

Whitetail deer make the trip from marsh to marsh as they travel from the mainland to the barrier beaches.

turned the vessel to head home. He never ventured that far from his home waters by boat again.

Any form of fishing is hunting at its finest. And fishing takes on many forms: crabbing, eeling, clamming, and something called *jacking*.

Historically, jacking involved anglers using a *cresset*—a metal container of oil, grease, wood, or coal burned as a torch mounted on a pole—to illuminate the bottom through shallow water from the bow of the boat. Modern jackers use a Coleman kerosene lantern, far superior in its brightness and fuel efficiency.

Pushing along from the bow with a twelve-foot pole, which had mounted on one end either a crab net or an eel spear, the jacker scanned the mud flats for blue crabs, eels, or flatfish like fluke and winter flounder.

Conditions needed to be just right for this activity. Darkness came first. These critters were far more active when the sun went down. Light to no wind was a must. One breeze and the surface wrinkled like a bed sheet left too long in the dryer. This distorted the bottom and visibility diminished. But foremost was the tide. It had to be low enough so the water could be seen through to the bottom and the net or spear could reach the crabs or eels hiding in the seaweed. But it also had to be high enough so the flat-bottomed boat could still pass over the sand bars and mud flats without getting hung up.

Once, around 1 a.m. while John III and Jeff II fished the flats in Baldwin Bay, a small pleasure cruiser struck the sandbar on the Baldwin side just east of the channel. The boaters' boisterous speech led the boys to believe alcohol played a major role in their poor navigation skills.

As John continued to fish and Jeff sorted the catch inside the boat, the unfortunate stranded souls saw the boys' lantern and called out. "We're stuck!"

The boys chuckled and shook their heads. They knew the rising tide would free the foolish weekend boaters soon.

The drunkards called out again, this time making their ignorance all too clear. "Is this the October tide?"

The boys burst into laughter. They didn't know if the boaters had referred to spring tides, neap tides, seasonal tidal fluctuations, or what. But they had certainly never heard of anything like an *October tide* before. And this was years before the Swedish death/doom metal band of the same name was created in 1994.

With all these conditions needing to be just right, you can imagine how many times a jacker will wake up after midnight, when the tide is just right, and then have to return home again because the wind picked up. That's why John's lone feat of bagging a doormat fluke was so amazing.

On this night, John jacked alone. And at thirteen years old, he had a lot of responsibility taking his garvey out in the dead of night by himself. He decided to skip crabbing and go for eels and fluke. His brother Mike had taken his own boat elsewhere that night for crabbing.

Sometime around 2 a.m., he wasn't having much success and figured he'd look solely for fluke on the edge of the sandbar where it dropped off into the deep navigational channel. No one jacked there but he knew people fished in the channel and in the hole in front of the nearby Port Williams bay house across from 998 Scow Creek. It made sense that there could be fluke on that transition between the shallows and the depths.

Frustrated and about to give up for eels elsewhere, he pushed off into the deeper water. Suddenly, the outline of an enormous fish appeared in about six feet of water, much deeper than the normal one to two feet he was used to. His heart raced because he thought he'd miss the shot due to the refracting light at that depth. Using most of the pole's length, he thrust the spear at his target.

When he pulled it up, he feared the massive fish would either fall off or jump out of the boat. So, he left it on the spear and shoved it partially under the bow. He fired up the engine and headed full speed, as any Combs would, back to the bay house. With a *Bang* into the dock, he tied up the boat and yelled, "I got a doormat!" He later admitted his real reason for waking everyone was to have witnesses. Fish stories are infamous at the bay house, and he didn't want to be part of one this day.

What struck them all as special, other than the fish's unusual size, was the near perfect spear strike across its gills, preserving the meat. The fish was so big it had to be fileted into quarters, each thick enough for a family dinner.

The next morning, John posed for the picture you see here. Peachy always had his 35mm Pentax camera with him and couldn't pass up the opportunity to record one of the largest flatfish ever caught on Scow Creek.

John E. Combs III, slayer of monster fish, c. 1984.

Five

Duck Tape

*W*hen it came to new discoveries while hunting, John's brother Mike had a flare for the dramatic. For months, he spoke of hunting ducks other than the standard mallards and black ducks that flew around Scow Creek. After a little research, he found that unique species called *sea ducks* often entered the Jones Beach Inlet. This treacherous channel separated the west end of Jones Beach and the east end of Point Lookout. These ducks sought the passage as a refuge from rougher seas offshore. But that didn't make the area safe for small vessels.

On this day, Mike ventured alone and piloted his small boat two and a half miles from the bay house to the inlet. After drifting silently in the choppy water for nearly an hour, his daredevil efforts paid off.

Mike raced back the bay house. He couldn't slow down over the mudflats so he kept the engine at full throttle, like any Combs would. The boat rammed into the dock with such a force that its bow shot upward and banged down onto a cleat punching a hole in the fiberglass coated plywood hull.

He ran into the bay house and woke everybody up to show them his colorful male surf scoter. This colorfully beaked species of duck looks like it took makeup lessons from both a circus clown and polecat, hence its nickname *old skunkhead*.

Later, Mike repaired his damaged hull with a one-foot square

A male surf scoter duck.

patch of plywood held on with roofing nails then sealed with duct tape and roofing tar. When he drove over waves for the rest of the boat's life, water shot like a fountain in short bursts into the air from the haphazard mend.

Jack in the Hole

*J*ack had an affinity for the sensational. Everything was a big deal. Even chastising one of the other guys for making a big deal was a big deal for Jack. He couldn't even say a cuss word without embellishment. Even his favorite expletive, "fahamsammich," wasn't an real expletive. "What the fa-HAM-sammich you do to your hair, Jimmy? You look like a flounder!"

Jimmy, Jack's youngest son, had recently gotten his hair frosted by his mother. She needed the practice. Actually, all the boys had their hair frosted by their mother but because Jimmy's was much shorter, it came out polka dotted. Jimmy was called "flounder head" for months.

Or "Where the fa-HAM-sammich you get that hunting coat from, Michael? Looks like somethin' outta the T.V. show *Bonanza*?"

Mike had somehow procured a hunting jacket that looked like a naval peacoat but mottled by odd squares of earthen hues of brown, orange, and green. It was forever dubbed *the Bonanza coat*.

This term had the momentary impression of it being a cussword, but then escalated into a humorous, yet harmless, exclamation.

One year, Jack brought out his brand new, semi-automatic, 12-guage shotgun. He had been so proud of this firearm and had high hopes of bagging his first duck in the marshes behind the bay house where the birds often swooped in to spend the night. In the pre-dawn mist, he snuck out the door while the rest of the hunters hadn't, as it's colloquially called, 'unassed the bed' yet.

Venturing into the bay alone on any given day poses its own perils. Walking in the marshes unaccompanied, in the dark, and with temperatures hovering around freezing only enhances the danger.

The sun would rise in about forty-five minutes, and Jack wanted to be in position before legal shooting time.

He walked past the trap shooting range behind the bay house. After stepping from the boardwalk, he entered the field of missed and broken clay pigeons causing his footfalls to emit strange crunching sounds as if he walked on a field of fortune cookies. After another minute, he passed a simple duck blind dubbed "The Lemonade Stand." Peachy used stakes and burlap cloth to create a camouflaged hideout from ducks. The only problem was its proximity to the bay house. Ducks typically steered clear of any large structures, so it was rare for them to land nearby. Jack needed to get farther away.

But he never made it to his previously scoped out spot. A few minutes later, Jack stepped into a natural pothole that swallowed him up to his neck. The only thing saving him from going all the way under was his brand-new shotgun. It stretched across the hole's opening from stock to barrel allowing Jack to eventually pull himself out. After traipsing back to the bay house in the twilight of dawn, he spent the rest of the day disassembling his firearm, cleaning all the mud and grass from it, and cursing his misfortune.

Later, the only thing Jack suffered were sore muscles and wise-cracks accusing him of attaching a *duskin' cork* to the end of his barrel to aid in shooting ducks in the dark. Historically, this practice was known as *dusking*. In the late 19th Century, market gunners would hunt at night with this rudimentary device, ultimately decimat-ing migratory bird populations. It was then made illegal. Of course, Jack hadn't practiced that behavior, but it didn't stop the incessant jocular-ity from his fellow duck hunters.

At 998 Scow Creek from left to right: Jack Combs, Jeff Keene Sr., and John Combs Sr. c. 1990.

Seven

Deep Trouble

When the boys became young adults, the adventures didn't stop. Since much of the surface of the bay had been explored, the next logical option was to go beneath the waves. Mike, John, and Surf all legitimately trained to use scuba gear. They used their certification to spear fish around bridge pilings.

The Meadowbrook and Loop Parkway bridges allow beachgoers and commuters passage over the scattered marshlands from the mainland to visit the famous Jones Beach and other barrier beach islands to the east and west. But they don't realize the perils lying below as they drive ignorantly overhead. The tidal current whips through these narrow corridors carrying with it dangerous debris and deadly creatures.

Mike and his friend, John Flemming, post-Hurricane Sandy co-lessee of 998 Scow Creek, liked to dive at night under the M-3 bridge (3rd bridge south of Merrick Road on the Meadowbrook Parkway) where blackfish (tautog) gather in large numbers. Only a three-mile trip by boat from the bay house, they frequented this overpass for its wide expanse and multitude of concrete pilings.

On one dive, Mike traveled near the bottom along a long horizontal cement block. A pit had been excavated beneath this structure by constant moving water. He had been there before because blackfish hung out in the cavity.

No fish this time. Only a foul penetrating submarine odor. So powerful was the stench that Mike smelled it through his mask. More like tasted it. He screwed up his face as much as one could when using a diving regulator. His flashlight pierced the rushing water, now strewn with white ghostly flakes of unknown origin.

He turned the corner of the block, and the light beam revealed a decaying whale carcass the size of a small car. Large pieces of flesh waved in the current and small fish schooled around it in a constant frenzy of feeding and fending off competitors.

The M-3 bridge had other secrets not meant for man's discovery lying in wait beneath its expanse. On another night dive for blackfish with Flemming, Mike found an odd *nub* sticking out of the sand. After getting Flemming's attention, they discerned the outline of a big fish and concluded through a series of hand gestures that the nub was part of an unknown-to-them species of fish.

Mike stretched back the elastic band of his spear gun and loosed the metal projectile into the buried fish's dorsal side. The bottom beneath them rippled and heaved. Up from the sand rose a giant ray with an eight-foot wingspan. Mike's spear had struck one of its wings.

The cartilaginous fish took off, dragging Mike behind it.

Flemming reached out and took hold of Mike's leg.

Mike tugged at the metal shaft of the spear trying to get it loose. After several minutes, he finally retrieved the small harpoon only to hear the buzzing of a boat's engine traveling above.

They resurfaced to find themselves halfway to the Jones Beach Inlet, one mile from the open ocean. They plodded along the surface, all the way back to the tethered boat, exhausted and utterly done fishing for the night.

This last diving story involves Surf accompanying Mike. Surf dove the first trip down, but the strong current had ripped his mask off, so he didn't go down for a second dive.

Mike exchanged air tanks and submerged once again. After several minutes, he surfaced to hand Surf a full bag of fish. With the blackfish, a bizarre gray creature poked its fins through the mesh. "Don't know what that is, Surf. But it's weird." Mike sunk back below and left Surf to ponder the unknown fish's identity.

Surf stared at the fish for some time. His wetsuit dripped onto the floor. An extra metal spear tip lay in the boat. He picked it up and poked the denizen of the deep in its head. It looked sad.

Or maybe it was angry.

A searing pain shot into Surf's hand, then up his arm and all the way to his shoulder. His whole appendage then went completely numb. He dropped the spear and panicked.

Mike resurfaced a few minutes later and tried to climb in the boat.

A northern stargazer.

Before he could, Surf yelled, "You better not go near that thing. It electrocuted me."

Mike burst into laughter. "What're you talkin' about? Nothin' happened to me when I touched it."

"It zapped me. I'm tellin' you."

Later, after searching in a book, they'd identified the fish as a northern stargazer. This creature uses its wormlike tongue to lure prey, has venomous spines, and, as Surf had been unfortunate enough to discover, can produce electric shocks upwards of fifty volts.

Due to a case of mistaken identity in murky water, the stargazer succumbed to its wounds. And Surf never poked a peculiar fish again.

Eight

Bird is the Word

*M*ystery presented itself every day in the bay. Nature's myriad of creatures, color, and cacophony of sounds lead one to ponder the Creator's astonishing miracles. Many of those sounds came from birds.

Anyone who has spent time outdoors on the south shore of Long Island has at least a minor familiarity with these species. Gwocks, medahens, and twiffle boids were the most common. What? You're not familiar with these common species? Let's take a closer look.

You're walking around the bay house. A flock of tiny birds approaches. Some dip under the house. Others chase each other as they circle the building twittering and chattering. These *twiffle boids* are actually barn swallows. But the name was used for any small chirping bird on the marsh.

One of the most haunting sounds on the bay after sunset is the American bittern. A particular note it creates resembles the sound made when driving a stake into the mud. Colloquially, it's called a meadow hen. But throw in a Long Island accent coupled with the salty spin *bay talk* puts on language, and the term *medahen* evolved. Medahen was also used to reference the clapper rail, a secretive bird related to cranes that also disrupts the blanketing quiet of the marshland.

Finally, the gwock is the most recognizable species, as its large size and often surprising vocal alarm will scare you when it flies up from a deep crick at low tide or jumps from a bulkhead on a trip through the canal. The term *gwock* was given to great blue herons, night herons, and any other bird producing that sound.

Of all these birds, the great egret stands out the most because of its bright white feathers. So when the boys saw one drifting down Scow Creek with the ebbing tide, they couldn't have imagined what they were about to discover.

They raced down to the floating dock.

Jeff reached into the water and grabbed one of its black legs. These birds stand over three feet tall. So, when he lifted it up, it took longer than they expected. As the bird's lengthy neck exited the water, Jeff felt it was too heavy. Something weighed it down.

Finally, the head emerged and the boys' mouths fell open.

A large quahog clam, still alive, had clamped onto the end of the egret's beak. The boys surmised that the hapless bird must have struck at a fish or worm and its beak entered an open clam in the mud. The clam's instinctual reflexes caused it to close tight.

The doomed bird must've fought for its life until succumbing to the inevitable.

Clams are strong. I've not met any person who could pry one open with their bare hands. You must use a special knife called, aptly, a clam knife. It has a relatively dull blade but just enough leverage to get between the interlocking shells, called valves, and cut the adductor muscle within. You could also steam them open. But predators have no such methods.

Seagulls will drop them on rocks, pilings, docks, and even the roof of the bay house. Sweeping up clam shells from the deck is a weekly chore. Sea stars use hundreds of tiny suction cups to force the valves open just enough to put their stomachs inside to digest the soft animal within. Humans harvest clams by digging them by hand or using a clam rake. They certainly wouldn't use a rod and reel. Well, not normally.

Mike, Jeff, and several of their teenage friends decided to play hooky one day on Mike's boat. They packed up snacks, bait, and gear and headed out. Somehow, a beer keg ended up onboard. They traveled through the bay, past the bay house, and stopped at the M-2 bridge to tie up.

Hours passed by and the boys passed out. When they woke, they reeled in their long forgotten baited hooks. Everyone pulled theirs up empty, with the bait stripped off long ago.

Everyone except Mike.

He struggled to free his line from an entanglement with the bottom. He cussed and complained and tried all the tricks to loose his hook. Finally, right before giving up and cutting it free, it slackened. He reeled it up. Dead weight slowed its ascent. Did he snag a horseshoe crab or a stingray? Maybe it was just a clump of sea lettuce.

As the end of the line broke the surface of the water, the boys couldn't believe their eyes. A large clam, just like the great egret, had clamped down on Mike's lead sinker. All his efforts must've loosened it from the sucking mud.

In all their years, they never heard of anyone catching a live clam with a fishing pole.

V

Ingenuity & Stupidity

Wind blows, scouring my paint and shingles. Rain pelts my surfaces and swells my wooden frame when it penetrates cracks. Ice freezes and expands, fracturing my window glaze. And insects, rats, and other creatures gnaw at my structure. The forces of both nature and repetitive use constantly wear me down over time. I need help from others to endure.

My stewards did not come from wealthy backgrounds. Anyone with financial freedom can buy the parts, lumber, and appliances to stay comfortable in a bay house. Nowadays, some bring solar panels, gas generators, and incinerating toilets to tackle the wild. Not my people. If it broke, they fixed me with what they could find. If it rotted or rusted, they replaced it with used new-to-me parts. And if a basic need went undelivered, they improvised, often to the nth degree and better than anything newfangled and store-bought.

But it's more than just the bay house. How would they access me without their boats and the motors to propel them? If not for the resourcefulness and creativity of my caretakers, I'd be left alone to collapse into a heap upon the marsh like so many other bay houses before me.

One

Ins & Outs

*P*henomena never ignored by people visiting the bay house are the weather, the tide, and the number of people passing in boats. Any idea to improve upon the recognition of, the deletion of, or the improving of these events was an idea worth exploring.

Gnats, greenflies, and mosquitos can plague visitors and even force them to vacate the bay house and go back home faster than they can say hydrocortisone cream. Sometimes, the gnats are so numerous they cover the giant spider webs slung across window-panes choking the jumbo predators' traps rendering them useless. The spiders abandon their posts and return only when the swarm abates. Knowing from the safety of the bay house's four walls if the wind has come to your aid in driving these bugs away came as great comfort to those who knew what to look for. A flying flag served well in this capacity.

The flagpole erected on the northwest corner of the deck had been created from an upcycled Town of Hempstead light post. Its aluminum length tapered

998 Scow Creek, pre-Hurricane Gloria (1985). The flagpole on the right and the 'tide o' meter' in the top left corner.

upwards where a welded ball of the same material sat adorned with the letters of the cardinal compass directions. Atop the ball, a metal arrow spun in the direction of the prevailing wind. A vane of such rudimentary magnificence could only be improved by the American flag flying below.

Tommy D. Seaman at 998 Scow Creek with the 'tide o' meter' in the background, c. 1984.

The pole served as a beacon to friends of the bay house. If the Stars and Stripes flew, it meant someone occupied the bay house. It meant conditions were suitable to stop by, say hello, and perhaps share a drink. A flying flag was the equivalent of Motel 6's "We'll leave the light on for you." But it could also mean, "The bugs aren't bad, so it's safe to visit."

The tide was another story. If conditions were right, it would work together with the wind to either drain the bay so greatly that every sand bar and mud flat was exposed or flood so high that every marsh island was nearly hidden. This had the effect of giving unwary boaters a false sense of depth. Many a weekend boater needed rescuing from running aground.

A friend of the bay house and all-around Mr. Fixit was Jeff "J.B." Blossom. A retired refrigerator repairman, J.B. possessed serious problem-solving skills. If there was some way to improve something, he got on it right away. You never had to ask. By simply observing the frustrations of others, J.B.'s mind started to work out the challenge. Within a few days, a contraption would show up and be installed, and everyone raved about its ingenuity. One of J.B.'s ingenious devices was the *Tide o' Meter*.

This gadget used the motion of moving water in the crick to

push a float tied to a pair of strings. The strings ran up a post to above the dock and were connected to a lever. Attached to the lever was a large metal needle painted red. When the needle moved, it pointed to either of two large letters: 'O' and 'I.' The 'O' stood for *outgoing* and the 'I' for *incoming*. With a good pair of binoculars, you could see which way the tide moved from as far away as the mainland. No more guessing if your boat would clear the sandbar or how long you'd have to wait until the tide turned to your favor. Remember, this was all before the internet and smartphone apps.

Another problem-solver was John Combs Sr. In the 1970s, at his bayhouse on Scow Creek just east of 998, a freshwater artesian well provided high-quality water for bathing, washing dishes, and cooking. But it was downright cold. And in the cooler months, showering proved impossible.

Providing warmer water in all seasons drove John Sr. to take the well water collection up a notch. After installing a 300-gallon tank on the top of the outhouse, he painted it flat black to absorb the sun's energy throughout the day. Cleaning off saltwater and mud from your body was never more enjoyable in the bay than in the shower that John built.

John Sr. knew about outboard engines too. On one opening day trip in 1975, he had some trouble after arriving at the bay house later than the rest of the men. Here is the conversation as recorded on cassette tape:

John Sr. stashed his gear near the couch where he always slept during group hunting trips. His son Jack hounded

Elizabeth "Betty Jean" Keene Engel on the marsh at Scow Creek c. 1978.

him for reasons why he was late. John started by describing his motor's diagnosis. "She started off. She stopped. I started her again. She stopped. She started and then I got down to the mouth [of the crick] and she just conked out, and that was the end of it."

Jack prodded for more information to help solve his father's engine problem. "You said she died even though you gassed her? That means she's loaded up with garbage."

"Nah, it's in the carburetor. Plenty of fire. I had enough fire to light up all of the canal."

Peachy knew the tape recorder was on and tried his best to get as much dialogue out of John Sr. as he could. "Maybe you got no plugs in the damn thing, and it's blowin' out the head."

John Sr. scoffed. "I even went home and poured five more gallon in another tank."

From the kitchen, Jack asked, "You used a different tank?"

"I used a different tank. Didn't make no difference."

Peachy suggested, "Maybe it's like Jack said and you need a new coil." At this point in the conversation, Peachy was trying to get John Sr. to say certain words as only John Sr. said them. For example, the word 'coil' was often pronounced 'curl' by the elder bayman.

This time, John Sr. wasn't taking the bait. "Not with the fire she's got, boy." His irritation grew with their questioning. "What do you mean, no plugs? Where do think I got the fire? Out a bull's ass?"

The guys erupted in laughter.

"When I shut my motor off, they shut the powerhouse off there was so much light around there."

Jack entered the main room. "You switched motors, too? What were you gonna do if the ten didn't work? Switch to the five?" He chuckled. "He degenerated from an 18 to a 10 to a 5. It'd take you to next Thursday to get out here!"

John Sr. even took his lawnmower out to the marsh. He swore it kept the bugs away by cutting the *Spartina* grass short in the summer months. It must have been some site when boaters of all sorts drove by and witnessed a man mowing the *lawn* around the bay house. The grandkids were happy about it when they played in the sandbox he had set up for them out there.

VI

As I've said, I'm no stranger to foul weather, and often the worst of its kind. Blizzards, ice storms, nor-easters, and hurricanes have battered my façade seasonally since my creation. But no time more than after I was placed out here on the marsh. Nature's relentless forces seek to destroy me every year and bring an end to my caretakers' ongoing experiences.

Sure, those forces ultimately did me in. But I exist more in a mystical sense, able to be reborn again and again, akin to a mythological phoenix. As long as my owners care enough about what I mean to them and their families, I'll always exist in one form or the next. For example, I now exist in the memories written in this book.

My caretakers know what they've got here. They know the physicality of my being is only temporary, but my spirituality is something altogether deeper and long-lasting. And only those who've experienced it firsthand can truly understand.

SLEEPING THROUGH THE STORM

The bay house is an amazing place to witness the weather. The wide-open space offers a three-hundred-and-sixty-degree unobstructed view of brilliant lightning storms flashing in the distance, creepy fog banks as they roll in, and magnificent sunrises and sunsets. People would pay a pretty penny for access to this vantage point and its unique experiences.

Being on the water and influenced by the Gulf Stream's ever-flowing tropical warmth, the accumulation of snow is a rare occurrence on the south shore marshes. But it does happen from time to time, especially during a blizzard. Accompanying this snowstorm was a westerly wind just strong enough to whistle as it blew through the unsealed cracks in the windowpanes.

Mike had been given the charge of sleeping on the couch downstairs so he could replenish the potbelly stove with wood several times during the night. Unfortunately for him, the couch laid directly beneath that exceptionally whistly window.

The Coleman lantern was turned low. Its soft hiss, along with the popping fire and howling wind, lulled everyone into a deep slumber. Mike was no exception.

The next morning, everyone woke to find their breath visible. The fire had gone out. When they went to wake Mike and complain about his poor stove-tending skills, they noticed something quite peculiar. Snow had entered through the crack in the window and deposited itself in a small drift across Mike's head and face.

He had slept soundly through the whole ordeal and almost didn't believe it when they told him. This was one of those times when a camera would have been a useful commodity.

ANCHORED TO THE OUTHOUSE

998 Scow Creek before Gloria made some design changes.
Notice the outhouse on the left.

ierce storms, although not commonplace in the bay, have left their
marks in more ways than one. Hurricanes, nor'easters, and blizzards rip,
shatter, and break shingles, planks, and windows with unrelenting force.

In 1985, Hurricane Gloria threatened Long Island. It had been
a Category 4 when approaching from the south. Panic struck as
the thought of what a storm surge from that magnitude of tropical
cyclone could do to the fragile, aging bay house.

Mike decided to act. But what could a lone seventeen-year-old
do in the face of the impending destruction of his family's property?
Tie the bay house to the outhouse, of course!

He didn't have an engineering degree or a contractor's license, so
we can excuse his lack of experience when deciding on such a course
of action. After all, what could anyone have done with the time and
resources at hand? At least he gave it a shot, albeit a futile one.

Mike gathered all the rope he could find and wrapped the
pilings of the larger structure to those of the smaller. Perhaps the

saying "built like a brick s***house" inspired him to use the diminutive building as an anchor. In any case, the deed was done. Ropes spread through doorways and windows. It looked as if a giant spider had taken a grand tour leaving its silky strands in every crevice and rafter.

Thankfully, the cooler North Atlantic water temperature had weakened Gloria to a Category 2 before its deadly eye passed directly over 998 Scow Creek on September 27, 1985. The resulting flood took the neighboring bay house off its foundation and used it as a battering ram. It floated by in the strong current, ripping the front porch of 998 clean off.

The tiny outhouse didn't have the might Mike had hoped for. The docks and decking were destroyed. And the bay house-to-bay house collision knocked the old barn off its pilings. It ended up sitting flat on the marsh several hundred feet to the west, flooded with mud, and nearly demolished.

Reconstruction began early the next spring resulting in some structural changes to the overall layout. The bay house still had another life in its allotment of lives. The height off the marsh increased, and a more open floor plan greeted visitors upon entry. 998 Scow Creek 2.0. The owners and their friends would have another twenty-six years of memorable experiences before the next fateful act of nature.

998 Scow Creek post-Gloria. Notice the front porch is missing.

Three

The House and the Hurricane

ℛecall the story in a previous chapter titled "Anchored to the Outhouse." After that debacle, the owners were thankful to get another two decades out of their beloved bay house, albeit rebuilt with modifications. Then came Sandy.

2012 brought a storm that would mean the end of many historic bay houses on the south shore of Long Island. Superstorm Sandy, a strong Category 2 when it struck Long Island, was the deadliest, most destructive, and most powerful storm of the season.

998 Scow Creek disappeared. Its fifty-year reign on the edge of the marsh had come to an end leaving behind sparse evidence of its existence. A few posts and sills remained where it once stood. Broken bits of glass and metal laid scattered amongst the broken lumber.

But its owners were not ready to give up.

Through a special dispensation by the Town of Hempstead, thanks in part to the heroic efforts of historian Nancy Solomon, bay house owners could rebuild on the same spot as their original house if the construction was completed within a five-year period. After that, if no one rebuilt, the land would be

A bay house razed by Hurricane Sandy, 2012.

left to return to nature, and the opportunity to lease would be lost forever.

The new leaseholders of Scow Creek, Mike Combs and John Flemming, sank pilings deep into the marsh, replacing the mud sills that failed to maintain the house's stability in the past two storms. They used new lumber, new nails, and didn't cut any corners in the construction. 998 Scow Creek had been born anew, ready to serve as a continued escape from the monotony of suburbia for a new generation of stewards lovingly known as *bay rats*.

The Seaman Family house lies in ruins under the M-1 bridge where the rising tide left it.

VII

*F*un, relaxation, and unforeseen adventures are the expectations when venturing to the bay house. Be it gatherings of family, parties with friends, or a deserted respite from the distractions of the mainland, I have served to fuel everyone's desires in all seasons.

It was always a treat to witness newcomers stepping from the boat to my dock. Their wide-eyed looks of wonder exhibited both excitement and trepidation. I enjoyed the questions I often overheard them ask.

"Where are all the trees?"

"Can you walk on the marsh?"

"Um, we have to use an out-*what* to go to the bathroom?"

Equally entertaining were my caretakers' skills at torture and harassment of these first-timers in the most inventive and unique ways solely for their personal pleasure.

But it wasn't just newbies who underwent the hazing so frequently applied by those experienced in the ways of the bay. Anyone was fair game, and games were all the rage at the bay house.

One

C.W.W.

*C*harles William Watson went by the name *Charley*, or to the kids *Uncle Charley*. This man, born on the 4th of July in 1908, served in the United States Navy and was present as a ground crewman when the German airship Hindenburg exploded over Lakehurst Naval Air Station in New Jersey in 1937. In historical footage of the incident, he was one of the sailors running for their lives as the giant zeppelin plummeted to the ground in a massive ball of flame.

In Freeport, New York, he worked as a civil engineer and was responsible for designing the layouts for many of the roads and storm sewer systems in the village. By the time he joined the Freeport Fire Department and the Fresh Air Gunnin' Club, he was considered a senior citizen at over sixty-years-old. But that didn't stop him from having a good time with the younger men at the bay house during hunting trips and competitive trap shoots.

The fastest way to get anyone out of a building is by filling it with smoke. In a real fire, the

Mike Combs, John Combs III, the author, and "Uncle Charlie," c. 1975.

circumstances are tense. Confusion ensues and panic follows. This is typically not considered to be a *good time*. But in this situation, the guys relished every mischievous minute.

Opening day eve for duck hunting season was the time to scout out potential hunting spots, prepare meals, and get everyone's gear organized for the next few days of lodging at the bay house. Everyone had a busy morning. This included Charley.

The fire in the potbelly stove had produced the perfect environment to counteract the chill in the late fall air that Charley's aging body was so susceptible to. He decided to take a nap on the couch.

Taking the opportunity, Jack decided to climb a ladder to the roof with an empty coffee can. He gingerly placed it on the potbelly stove's galvanized metal chimney to block the escaping exhaust. The resulting back draft sent smoke on a reverse path through the pipe charging the entire living area with thick gray soot.

Charley woke to find the haze of sleepiness had been trumped by the near zero visibility of actual smoke before his eyes. He found his way to the stove through a maze of furniture. "What's wrong with this thing? Someone must've closed the flue." He coughed while wrestling with the iron contraption.

The guys looked through the windows from on the deck and couldn't stop laughing.

Charley was such a good sport. Once he found out nothing was wrong with the stove, he exited and laughed right along with them.

Until the next hunting trip.

As an old-timer, Charley had more routines than the younger guys. One of those practices was always having his slippers lined up and readily available on the floor next to his side of the bed. It makes sense, especially when the floor is cold or full of splinters like the deck of the bay house.

Charley woke as he always did to start the day, excited for the chance at bagging some birds. Upon sitting bedside, he slid his feet into his slippers and stood. Then he couldn't move his legs. He pulled and yanked, but his feet wouldn't leave the floor.

The guys had nailed his brand-new slippers down to the lino-leum-plywood floor. They all slept through it and missed out on the moment, but Charley filled them in afterwards. He laughed right along with them.

Until the next hunting trip.

Charley had worn corrective lenses for most of his adult life. And like everyone who depends on their glasses, he took them off and placed them on the nightstand before going to bed.

Peachy's profession was that of optician. As such, he had access to numerous types of lenses and frames, some of which matched nearly as close to Charley's as the originals. So, while Charley slept, Peachy switched his spectacles with a set containing lenses with a prescription far from that upon which Charley relied to see clearly.

Charley woke in the early morning hours to relieve himself outside over the railing, as was the practice. He looked out over the marsh toward Point Lookout, a beach hamlet on the barrier island to the south. The most visible landmark there was the lollipop-shaped water tower. In the dark, its blinking red light warned aircraft of its presence.

Charley had to look twice at the towering structure in the distance. He closed his eyes, shook his head, and looked again. There they stood. Two water towers, one above and slightly to the side of the other.

He then looked down at his manhood. Two of them also. Something was definitely wrong with his eyes. He hadn't had enough to drink the night before to produce this much double vision. It must have been his glasses.

Peachy and the rest of the guys woke shortly thereafter and all laughed at the innocent prank over breakfast.

Until the next hunting trip.

This final C.W.W. story, a special rendition obtained from an actual 1977 cassette tape recording as Jack Combs tells it, gives a verbatim first-person account of yet another practical joke played on innocent Charley. All involved were present at the time of the recording. But this time, the ruse involved a taxidermied pheasant and the discharge of a firearm.

Peachy: "So, what was the funniest thing that happened out here so far on this trip?"

Jack: "I think the best thing was Charley with that bird. 'Cause we played that up to the hilt. They went out there and put it out there. I went out there and played along to see if there was anything out there. Peachy wanted to do it right away. I says, 'No, no, no. Wait, wait.' Once he [Charley] sat down, we're all sitting around, and I got up and looked out the window and said, 'Dammit, there he goes. There he goes.'"

Charley: "And I heard eem."

Jack: "Tommy said, 'Uh, oh. I know it's going off now.' I ran to that window over there and said, 'There he is! He lit right, right there.' Tommy and Richie run for the gun case to get their guns. I run out outside and say, 'No wait, wait, wait, a minute. Who didn't get no bird? Charley! Charley didn't get no bird. Let Charley have a shot. Let Charley have a shot.' Charley gets his gun and loads it up. I says, 'Somebody get a gun. Back eem up just in case.'"

Peachy: "Mush is in here pissin' in his pants."

All the guys laugh.

Jack: "So, Charley walks up to the railing and says, 'Oh, oh, oh, yea. Oh, yea. I see him.' He raised his gun. I say, 'Charley, you better give it him before he gets up. Let him have it, Charley.' WHAAAM!"

All the guys erupt in laughter once more.

Jack: "Medahs blew up all over the place and the bird just sat right there, like that." He pointed to a stuffed pheasant on a shelf attached to the wall.

Charley: "I said, 'That sombitch didn't fall over.'"

Tom: "Mush was in here bustin' a gut. I thought he'd wet himself."

Mush: "I had a bellyache, laughing. I'm surprised you didn't give him the other barrel. Would've tore him right loose."

Jack: "It would've been nothing but sawdust."

Mush: "I'll say one thing, Charley. Your bird looks pretty good sittin' up there."

Charley: "Doesn't it?"

Mush: "Not too many guys can say they shot a bird and had him stuffed all in the same day."

Charley: "That's an accomplishment."

Two

GET OFF MY LAWN!

$\mathcal{S}$ummertime brings out the weekend boaters. Think of what *Sunday driver* means to most people and apply that to those who own oversized boats, have limited maritime navigation experience, and even more limited understanding of what it takes to be a responsible boater.

With all the boats gathered at the bay house, the incessant waves from large vessels passing by drives the boats into each other. It takes an engineer to calculate the tide and wind while tying the boats perfectly so none bang into the floating dock or each other. No such people ever visited the bay house, so the boats got jostled quite a bit. The bay house visitors couldn't take any more. It was time to rebel against these weekend cabin cruiser jockeys.

Peachy, having served in Vietnam, had an affinity for explosives. In the 1980s, large firecrackers known as M-80s and *blockbusters* were easily obtained, if one knew the right people. Every year, right before Independence Day, these illegal 1/8th and 1/4th sticks of dynamite *fireworks* became plentiful. Peachy often brought out several for everyone's entertainment. He was mischievous to the point of evil genius.

He had made stationary incendiary devices in the past out of old gasoline tanks and one of these explosive devices. If you leave just enough gasoline in the tank and place it in the sunlight for a few hours, a high density of vapor builds up inside. He then taped a blockbuster to the side of the tank. A lit cigarette served as the perfect slow timer. As the cigarette burned down, it eventually ignited the fuse, and *WAHFOH!* The shock wave rattled the windows. These entertaining devices were colloquially called *dago bombs*. (See the glossary at the end of the book for etymology.)

On a particularly busy holiday weekend one summer, the cabin cruisers and party boats passing the bay house grew to unhealthy numbers in the narrow channel. Some of the vessels sped along throwing dangerous wakes. Peachy had enough of it.

Skipping the tank of gasoline, he simply taped a cigarette timer to a blockbuster and attached them to a piece of Styrofoam the size of a small briefcase. Realizing the wind and tide were just right to carry the floating munition right into the channel, he released it from the bay house's floating dock.

It took about twenty minutes for the booby-trapped raft to reach the marine traffic lane. As a large party boat approached, music blaring and waves crashing into the marsh banks, the guys in the bay house knew the timer would be close to ignition. Just twenty feet from the vessel's hull, the firecracker detonated.

Pieces of white polystyrene and seawater flew into the air. The passengers on the vessel had no idea what happened. And the guys at the bay house couldn't stop laughing at their tomfoolery.

Three

A Bird in the Hand is Worth Two in the Marsh

$\mathcal{O}$ver the years, the bay house served as an escape for the firemen of Freeport Hose Company #1 to hold their annual *Bay House Party*. Long awaited and heavily planned, this event involved a serious traditional activity: The Snipe Hunt.

Initiating new members of the firehouse was a tradition. And, as always, the initiate must prepare themselves mentally for the punishment to come. Traditionally, the newbie has no idea what to expect, as the initiators remain tight-lipped. Except for the buildup.

They are made aware some adventure awaits when entering this virtual jungle realm called the marshland. They're told it's a wild place full of dangers most could never imagine and few would ever dare to venture. Of course, most of it was true, but it's played up to the nth degree. The cherry on top is the anticipation of the great snipe hunt.

This elusive, but real bird is touted to be fast, hard to see, and a great pairing with chicken eggs for a delicious breakfast. They are legal to hunt, but you'd need half a dozen or so to feed one person. Individual birds usually sit tight until suddenly flushing near your feet, flying off in fast zigzags. This, and other actual behaviors, make the snipe the perfect target for the hunt. A target that will never suffer any pain because the bird will never be caught by the clueless hunter.

Customarily, this right-of-passage hunt requires the initiate to venture into the woods or empty field with nothing but a source of light and a burlap sack. They are then made to call the words "snipe, snipe, here snipe" over and over until the bird comes to them. Their only impossible goal? To catch a snipe in the sack. But there are many adaptations. Here's the bay house version: add alcohol (lots of it), a custom-made sniping stick—a three-foot-long 2x4 board with a carved handle on one end and the words 'SNIPE STICK' scrawled on the blade—, a weak flashlight, and deep crick mud. This was the recipe for a howling good time.

Whether a new firefighter or a teen in the Explorers program (sans alcohol), the result was the same—confusion, adrenaline, and ending up to their waist, stuck in the mud.

It helped when a conspirator egged on the initiate with taunts and cajoles.

"He's over there! In the grass."

"He just ran across that crick."

"What do you mean, you *didn't* see him!'"

Once they tried to ford the crick, the flashlight became covered in mud, the snipe stick floated away, and the hunt ended abruptly with calls for help in the dark by the hapless victim.

Mission accomplished. Memories made.

VIII

CONVERSATIONS, RECOLLECTIONS, & POETIC CREATIONS

*T*hese stories about me are a culmination from a great variety of resources. It's a shame many other conversations on so many other days have been lost to the passage of time. Stories of love and heartache, successes and failures, and even those of life and death, all absorbed by my walls and into the fabric of my very being. If all the stories had been written, they'd fill untold volumes. Combine those with the stories of all the other bay houses on the south shore of Long Island and a veritable library could be built. They'd call it *The Repository of Bay House Narratives* or something equally fanciful and noteworthy.

One of the resources you'd find in the *reference* section of the imaginary repository would be a set of cassette recordings of visitors created by the author and his father in 1975, 1977, 1991 and 1995. Their rare testimonies color the pages of this memoir anthology. The following two excerpts are transcripts from the 1991 recording. Following them are individual memories from some of the people blessed enough to have visited the bay house in their time.

One

Eleven people slept over this late November night before opening day for duck, and the house bustled with pre-hunt activity. Peachy looked around at the lively crew and called from across the large central multipurpose room. "Hey, Jack! Imagine we all had 'bout eight kids each."

Jack surveyed the scene as well. "Where *did* all these kids come from?"

Everyone chuckled.

Tom Seaman moved one of the boy's duffle bags from a captain's chair in the corner and sat with a grunt. "Used to be just the four of us out here. *Now* look at the place."

Mike Combs had been sitting at the table. His knee still ached from a recent ligament surgery. "Every father, except Peachy, got two kids out here now."

Jeff Keene II scoffed at Mike's statement. "You all gotta be so promiscuous."

Mike smirked, took a swig of his drink, and looked at his father, Jack. "Wait till we *all* have kids. A million of 'em."

Jack produced a deriding hiss from between his teeth. "You gonna look for me and Uncle Peach, Uncle Tommy, and Uncle Rich. We'll be over in the West . . . I mean East Bay."

Mike smiled wryly back. "Yea, you'll be in the West Bay, all right. On the dumps!"

Jeff glanced through the window toward the setting sun to see the mountain of garbage to which Mike referred in the town of Oceanside silhouetted against the Manhattan skyline.

Peachy's face became contemplative. "I left a sock on my foot one night. That's why I got a girl."

Jack turned to go back into the kitchen. "That's your problem."

Tom pointed accusatively at Peachy. "I told you 'bout that."

Mike, having already had his first child, a girl, replied. "I didn't have no socks on."

Two

Fuel for Thought

The guys had configured their sleeping arrangements by choosing which bed to sleep in, stowed their clothes, and placed their unloaded shotguns in the rack on the wall near the door. The younger generation played cards at the central dining table while the dads sat in the comfortable hand-me-down chairs and couches on the perimeter of the great room. The fire crackled in the woodburning stove while wavelets lapped against the hulls of the boats moored out front. The bay house smelled of garlic and other Italian spices after the men devoured bowls of mounded spaghetti and meatballs.

Jack addressed his longtime friend and fellow firefighter Tom Seaman. "If we're gonna take a ride, we better go in the next half hour."

Tom crossed his legs and stretched them out. "Go where? What for? I'm content."

Mike contemplated the cards in his hand. "I'll take bets on this you don't go nowheres."

Tom gave Mike an incredulous look. "Don't make bets. Then I'll *have* to do it."

John Combs Sr. took a sip of his tea and said, "You're right then, Tom."

Jack ignored the counterarguments. "Sure you don't wanna take a ride then, Tom?"

"Where the hell we gonna go?"

John Sr. put his tea down on a side table. "You don't wanna scare the boids up. Leave 'em set."

To which Peachy added, "What birds? We just poisoned 'em all burnin' the garbage."

Three

The Bayathlon

*T*his story was originally written by the author when he was a senior at Freeport High School. His film studies teacher, Ms. Arlene Adel-Posses, assigned the creation of an original screenplay. He adapted one from a personal experience on the bay but had spun a tale full of embellishments, including a daring water rescue by the U.S. Coast Guard.

Years later, a more factual narrative was published in the Fall 2016 Long Island Traditions newsletter with the subtitle, 'A true story about youth, impulsiveness, and luck on the south shore of Long Island,' accompanied by a misspelled title. The author regrets having been unable to edit the story before publication but has since corrected that in the more candid rendition below.

As teenagers, Jeff and his cousins, Mike and John Combs, had planned to do this incredible feat they jokingly referred to as *the bayathlon* for several weeks. The bayathlon, as defined by the boys, involved traveling to their family's bay house without the use of a boat. The bay house, like others of its kind, sat quite some distance from the mainland. Without a vessel, swimming and *marsh-hopping* were the only ways to accomplish it.

As summer waned, they finally decided to meet on the bulkhead at the south end of Lester Avenue in Freeport. The boys were born and raised in this town. The bay was in their blood, and this bayathlon seemed like one more way to get some more of that bay to course through their veins.

It wasn't an effortless journey. Nearly a mile and a half of treacherous landscape awaited them. At times one would have to swim for fifteen minutes to get to an island or a sandbar, then hike across the muddy marsh, littered with sharp clam shells and deep holes, to where the water began again. Navigational channels and strong currents would need to be overcome. Add to that no drinking water, hats, or sunscreen were brought along. The challenges were real.

Mid-morning met the boys with bright sunshine and warm air. They readied themselves to jump in by tightening the laces on their bay sneakers and bathing suit waistbands. Bay sneakers were either those shoes bought for the prior school year, worn out by daily P.E. classes and hikes through suburbia, or off-brand kicks gifted by their non-hip grandmother that were too embarrassing to wear to school or anywhere else in public.

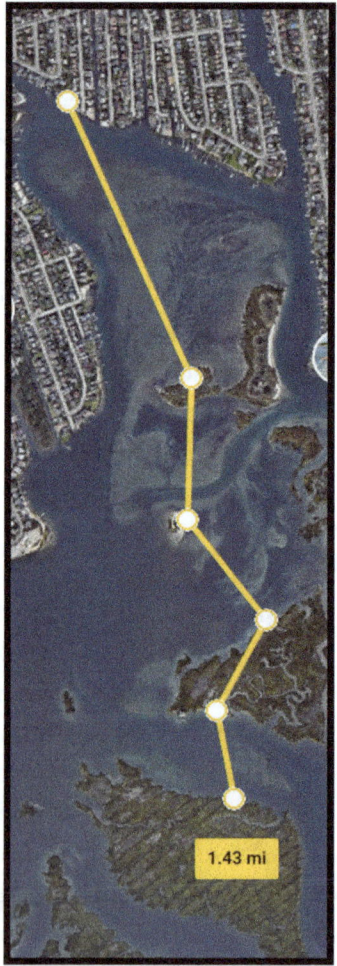

Sunlight glistened on the windswept water. The big decision. Who goes first? They decided all should hold hands and leap in together.

Calm, cool, incoming tide water washed away August perspiration. After getting their bearings, the first leg of the journey began. Heading south, they swam for about ten minutes across a channel to reach the first sandbar. The tide had receded, so traversing this second obstacle should've been easy. These long, usually narrow, ridges of built-up sand and sediment often spell disaster for unwary boaters who run aground upon them. But for our three adventurers, it was a welcome change to the swim they just endured. Not being trained swimmers, they relied on these respites to wade toward their

The boys' path as they conquered the first ever bayathlon.

destination. But this tract was nearly a half mile long and their energy quickly diminished.

As they exited the water at the first marsh island, they looked off into the distance. The bay house still seemed quite far. The tide inched higher and higher and the wind picked up ever so gently. After resting at the southern bank of this small island for a few minutes, their trepidations became evident when no one cared to reenter the water.

Mike, the oldest, made up the others' minds by pushing John into the water.

Mike Combs unhooks a fish from the author's pole while Brian Laudman looks out across the water at Wink Carmen's bay house, c. 1979.

A submerged obstacle scraped the top of John's foot and he scolded his brother for his tormenting behavior.

Mike and Jeff entered afterward and coaxed John to continue ahead regardless of his affliction.

It took another two hours of doggie-paddling over seaweed strewn mudflats and strenuous plodding through salt meadows to reach the lonely bay house.

The boys scrambled up the marsh bank and climbed the stairs to the deck of the bay house. Bits of green paint peeled from the trim and flaked off when they searched for the hidden door key under a warped windowsill.

Mike started a cozy fire in the wood-burning stove. They welcomed the warmth and used it to heat up some canned soup their family stored for hunting trips and other outings. Three hours passed while the boys rested and played card games at the Formica dining table.

The time to clean up and head back had arrived while plenty of daylight remained. But the wind had grown stronger and the tide had risen well above the sandbars, affectively turning wading into full-on swimming.

To make matters worse, exhaustion had crept up on them and they realized the daunting task ahead no longer held the enticement it had earlier that day.

As with all bay-raised children, improvisation was an acquired and necessary skill. So the three boys decided to fashion a sailboat from a large piece of Styrofoam stored out back. They found a bed sheet for the sail and lumber for the mast and rudder.

By the time the boys had constructed their makeshift vessel, the tide achieved its strongest current. They decided not to pass up the opportunity. However, the northwest wind countered the tide's advantage, and northwest was the very direction they needed to go to reach the closest part of the mainland just over a half mile to south Baldwin.

Sailing had not been any of the boys' fortes. So tacking proved a fatal maneuver. A sudden gust toppled the keelless craft when they had traveled only an eighth of mile to the mainland.

Mike and Jeff maintained their grip upon the water-logged craft.

But John was swept away by the current. His injured foot hampered his ability to stay close the other boys.

Mike and Jeff tried with all their might to right the sailboat but the cloth sail had soaked up water like a sponge. They abandoned the short-lived craft and, along with John, did their best to make for

The author (foreground) and John E. Combs III at Wink Carmen's bayhouse, c. 1975.

the marsh across the crick from the bay house. From there, the swim would have been three tenths of a mile.

If their situation didn't appear dire enough, thunderclouds loomed in the distance. Just as things seemed darkest, a small boat approached from up shore. Mike and John's father, Jack, headed out to the bay house to drop off supplies and happened to notice the boys stranded on the marsh.

They waved frantically for his attention.

Once he saw them, he pulled up and allowed them to climb onboard.

They thanked him profusely. Later, they realized how fortunate they'd been and how grateful they were for the wisdom gained while attempting this dangerous and unprecedented stunt.

Four

998 Scow Creek

a poem by the author, c. 1990

Here it was where we grew up
Never knowing what the future held.
Until one day the hurricane hit
Reducing the house to a shell.
With hard work and lots of time
The bay house near complete,
The past restored, the future assured
With feelings hard to beat.
Through parties and picnics, vacations, and hunts
To injuries, accidents, and break-ins by punks.
It's lived through it all, this house we adore.
To keep coming back, we'd wish this some more.
It's our kids who return to take our place.
Like generations before, to the bay house let's race!
In this last stanza we'd like to toast
For here is where we wish to be the very, very most!

Five

a poem by the author, c. 1990

Blood, sweat, and tears
Went into making this place.
And through all the years
We welcomed every face.
So, if in your heart
You're compelled to return
Please resist the urge
To break, steal, or burn.
The fire is warm.
The blankets are dry.
If one does no harm,
The limit's the sky!
And always remember
This house remains here
From October to September
Of every year.
Now, when the sun sets
The day, it is done,
Please don't forget
That we've got a gun!

Six

I grew up out there with my parents. Then married my husband, who also grew up out there. He, in turn, raised his three sons on the bay. Knowing we were all considered bay rats, we would eat and live from its bounty. Clamming, fishing, jacking for crabs and eels, and harvesting mussels.

Someone always stopped by, either friends or people needing help. Even the police, from time to time, to have a drink or something to eat, or maybe just to say hi. All were welcomed. But you had to have a boat.

Everyone took the sunsets for granted . . . with the skyline of the Twin Towers, the Empire State and Chrysler Buildings.

Then, 9/11/01 happened. When the towers fell.

I was on my way to work. I heard the sorrowful news report describe one of the towers had been hit by a plane. As I reached work, a second plane hit the other tower. At that point, I knew we were under attack. I called home. Jack was on his way to go clamming. I told him to turn on the news before he went to see what was going on.

I then called a friend and told her to turn on the news. Her husband Lou was already out in the bay. She called and told him to look towards the city.

He said it was very eerie. Smoke rose from the towers. He had no idea one of them made ready to collapse.

Another friend, Irv Morgan, called. He said his son called from the city asking to be picked up. He asked if he and Jack could come in by boat. But he had been told they wouldn't be able to get near any of the piers.

Jack made his way out to the bay just in time to see the terrible ordeal unfold before his eyes.

When I got home from work, we went out to sit at the bay house to watch the smoke rise from where the Twin Towers had once stood. A very sad sight. We will never see them again. Never see the horizon the same while the sun sets devoid of their magnificence.

PERSONAL STORIES
Story from Brendan A. Combs

The somber remains of 998 Scow Creek after Hurricane Sandy, Fall 2012.

*R*ight after Hurricane Sandy, I went out to survey the damage at the bay house. Where the bay house . . . was. Everything inside worth keeping was gone or destroyed. Nothing of the house remained but the mud beneath and some wood sticking out of the marsh.

While policing the grounds for anything worth salvaging, I found two miraculous items: a memorial firefighter plaque and an enormous quahog clam shell upon which was written, "Dug by Jack Combs."

Nine years before the storm, I lost my grandfather, Jack Combs, caretaker and steward of the bay house. *Pop Jack*, as we called him, would have been devasted at its loss. Perhaps these keepsakes, the only objects I found that day, are his way of saying he's still out there, watching over that very spot.

Memorial plaque found in the mud by Jack Combs' grandson, Brendan Combs, after Hurricane Sandy destroyed the bay house.

PERSONAL STORIES
Story from James "Jimmy" D. Combs

When I was a little boy, my father let me build small platform forts on the marsh. I used the not-so-good planks from the bay house wood pile. Then, he would make me tear it down, always saying, "We don't need any trouble from the authorities about new structures being built."

So, I would tear it down and a week or so later do it again. This, I believe, is where my skills to build with wood and other materials blossomed to what it is today. I miss him sometimes, and I like to remember the good things like this. I'm not even sure he realized what he did for me when he let me do those things at the bay house.

PERSONAL STORIES
Story from Ricky "Surf" Laudman

*M*e, my little brother Brian, my cousin Tommy Novotny, and Kevin Rooney took my garvey, Mr. Crab, to a small island we passed every trip from the house on the mainland to the bay house. This island had an inviting sandy beach we frequented in the summer. Firecrackers were the pastime of many kids, and we proved no different. We lit a small fire on the island to ignite the firecrackers left over from Independence Day. They had short fuses, so we threw them into the fire to prevent them from blowing up in our hands.

I took my eyes off the fire for a moment. When I turned back around, sparks had jumped to the dry marsh grass. The flames grew to more than twenty feet high in the hot summer air. We threw water from a bucket we kept on the boat for crabbing but it made no difference.

Brian got too close and singed the eyebrows clean off his face. That scared me enough to abandon the island and get home fast.

The fire eventually burned itself out, as the small island sat far away from other sources of fuel. But not before depositing heavy gray ash over the entire adjacent neighborhood.

Personal Stories
Story from Elizabeth (Stuerzel) Helsel

Some of my best childhood memories are from growing up on the bay and spending time out there with family and friends. We experienced something most people never do. And for that, I am forever grateful. We have the salt in our blood. I wish my children had that.

PERSONAL STORIES
Story from Linda (Combs) Stuerzel

The one thing that sticks out in my mind is when everyone would have games of catch in the water with clams we dug up from the mud. I especially think about the time Miguel [Bermudez] got hit while playing. Somehow, the impact dislocated his shoulder. They had to take him by boat to Waterfront Park in south Freeport where an ambulance took him to the hospital.

Personal Stories
Story from Denise (Schimmel) Layden

I remember one time being at the bay house overnight. We woke up, and Mush made pancakes. They were huge, and I didn't understand why. But when I asked for another, he replied, "One per man."

I also remember pushing my sister Anne off the edge of the dock. Her feet were under the top rung of an old metal ladder. She came up out of the water crying. The ladder had scrapped the front of her ankles.

Also, I hated using the outhouse. I was afraid to go back there. I felt like I was going to get swallowed up somehow.

My sister Anne's memories are of the yummy homemade Manhattan clam chowder Jack used to make. And when she wasn't wearing sneakers in the water and cut the bottom of her foot. My dad had to take her back to the mainland to be treated at the hospital.

The author's sister, Elizabeth "Betty Jean" Keene Engel, using the outhouse. c. 1971.

My sister Debbie's memories are of walking behind

the bay house at low tide and searching for anything and everything interesting. There was also the time we rode in a long rowboat to get out there. My Uncle John [Schimmel] sat in front, and when my dad [Rod Schimmel] got into the back, it started filling with water from the side, and we almost capsized. Uncle John said, "Rod, what are ya' trying to do? Kill us all!" But we hadn't left the dock yet and I'm sure it wasn't deep.

PERSONAL STORIES
Story from Steve Trimboli

I proposed to my wonderful wife, Pamela, at the bay house. True story.

But first things first, I had to buy a diamond. So, I studied diamonds and I knew everything I needed in order to get the right stone. A few days later, I jumped on the Long Island Railroad with a pocket full of cash and headed to the Diamond District in Manhattan. It took me most of the day shopping around, in and out of jewelry stores. The first few jewelers tried to sell me crap, so I picked up an eyepiece from a corner store. Suddenly, jewelers were showing me the good stuff. I picked up the perfect stone. Later, Downtown, I ended up in a basement where I had a jeweler make me the perfect setting to match.

On the way home, I stopped at Yia-yia's house. I needed to show her grandmother the ring. I had great respect for this amazing woman. After tearing up she said, "Good luck." And yes, they were tears of joy.

Earlier that day, I had borrowed Mike's [Combs] duck boat, covered in salt hay, to bring Pamela's brother, Jimmy, out to the bay house. Jimmy was going to school to be a chef, and an amazing one at that. We loaded the boat up with a bunch of goodies and headed out to the bay house where we worked together to create a romantic setting. Wine, music, a tablecloth, even candles. I had him cook up her favorite dish, and he made it real fancy. Then, I shot him back to my brother's house on the water in Freeport. I left the duck boat there.

It so happened my brother's roommate, Boli, had his birthday the same week. They had planned a party at his house with most of our mutual friends that same night. So we got together and made it a double birthday party. The only difference was Pamela's big surprise.

It was a cold night in late November. I picked Pamela up in my '85 Mustang GT. We arrived at my brother's dark and seemingly desolate house with a surprise night out in the duck boat. She hesitated at first but back then all I had to do was ask twice. She jumped right in the boat with me. She had no clue what was going on. We got in the duck boat and headed out into the brisk bay. If my memory serves, the air temperature was about 35 degrees Fahrenheit. Ice floated in the creek.

About half an hour later, Pam and I arrived at the bay house just as the sun was going down. I had it lit up before she arrived, and it looked so nice as we pulled in. We enjoyed a wonderful meal and an equally excellent bottle of wine.

Afterwards, I brought her out on the dock. At the same time, we both noticed how wonderful the moon lit up one side of the bay house. I turned around, got down on one knee, and made my move.

Pamela Trimboli around the time this story took place. Mike's duck boat, without salt hay, is on the right.

I remember not believing how much I surprised her. I honestly thought she might've known it was coming. We were together for years at that point, and I was not going to let her get away.

So after some kissing and cuddling we made our way back to the duck boat and off we went back to what she thought was an abandoned house. Meanwhile, it was packed with seventy partying people.

When I got in the canal, I picked up my Microtech Motorola flip phone and called my brother's house. "The bird is in the nest." That was the queue to shut the lights and turn off the music.

My fiancée looked at me. "What the hell was that about?"

I said nothing.

We pulled up to the pitch-black house. Upon entering, the lights went on, and all our friends let loose, "Happy birthday!"

She was blindsided. A perfect ending to a perfect night.

I have a picture of her in the doorway practically crying with her shining new engagement ring.

The bay house has meant so much to us over the years. I tried buying one many times. A very difficult thing to come across. It is what it is. At least I have good memories of the one on Scow Creek.

PERSONAL STORIES
Story from Brian J. O'Hare

I remember Jeff Sr. and one of the other guys put duck wings on a stuffed turtle. He said, "Come out and look what we shot." It had been laid on the picnic table, and it looked so real, like something out of a children's fantasy book. We were all like, "What is that?!" Plain as day, he said, "It's a morphydite." I've been using that term for years because of that story.

Personal Stories
Story from Fred Ledetsch

At a gun club trap shoot in the '80s, Andy Yankus Jr. had supplied the breech of his shotgun with a reloaded shell. Normally, this wouldn't be a problem. But this particular shell, unbeknownst to Andy, was reloaded with a double amount of powder. Lucky for everyone else, he was in the first position on the shooting platform with no other shooters adjacent. When he pulled that trigger, the gun's rear end blew up. By the grace of God, no one was hurt.

IX

*Y*ou've heard of *pirate talk*. And perhaps you're familiar with *valley girl talk*. But many, unless they've spent time under my roof, have probably never been exposed to *bay house talk*.

Often, it can seem as foreign as trying to understand Cockney English, but bay talk is based upon everything from a crude understanding of taxonomy to an even more unrefined sense of grammar and diction. Some spoke it regardless of their location, carrying the colorful metaphors with them to the grocery store, to school, to church, or to family holiday dinners. Others were more adaptable and saved it specifically for being on the bay when not in mixed company.

Regardless, the colloquialisms outlined below are the informal declarations that help define the whole experience of being from and of the bay. I hope you enjoy them.

key: n. – noun, v. – verb, i. – idiom

2 x heavy – n. [too bahy HEV-ee]
    any exceptionally thick, long plank used in decking or sills of a bay house, often found washed up on the marsh and used second-hand; the actual dimensions are unrelated to the term
    Example: *Grab a couple of 2 x heavies off the back rack so we can fix this rotting deck.*

brown sugar – n. [broun SHOOG-er]
    1. any liquor in a brown bottle, typically rye whiskey

2. a way of expressing the desire for another drink in mixed company

Example: *Hey, pass a glass of that brown sugar down here.*

burnin' barrel – n. [BUR-nin BAR-uhl]

either a 55-gallon drum or galvanized steel mesh garbage bin placed fifty-feet from the bay house and used to dispose of refuse, often producing a column of black smoke and typically visible for ten or more miles. (see 'white gas')

Example: *Quick, get those empty lead shell boxes in the burnin' barrel before the bay constables show up.*

California dew – n. [kal-uh-FAWRN-yuh doo]

1. used to describe a light rain event
2. also called a 'dry spell of dampness'

Example: *We can't go out in this rain. Sure, you can. It's just California dew.*

couple minoots – i. [KUHP-uhl min-OOTS]

1. attributed to the desire to linger a while longer at the bay house before heading up shore; can result in an actual couple of minutes and range upwards of an hour
2. pronounced by most people as 'a couple of minutes' or 'a couple of minutes more'

Example: *Hey, you guys ready to go? To which they'd reply, "Couple minoots" and pour themselves some more brown sugar.*

crick – n. [krick]

1. any serpentine natural body of water varying in size from a few feet to several hundred feet across. E.g., Scow Crick or Turtle Crick
2. called a 'creek' by most people

Example: *Why don't you boys go jump in the crick once more before we head up shore?*

D'agastino – n. [DAG-uh-steen-oh]

1. an old nail hammered straight to be used again (see 'nagel')
2. most likely a derogatory term

Example: *Hand me a few more of those D'agastinos so's I can secure this 2 x heavy.*

dago bomb – n. [DEY-goh bom]

1. term for a very loud firework, often without color and meant for sound effect only; derived from the fact that the best firework shows in America were historically Italian-American creations
2. most likely a derogatory term

Example: *Peach, you better be careful with those dago bombs your setting out on the marsh.*

dead bird never falls out of its nest – i. [I just can't even . . .]

1. used by George "Mush" Carmen on many occasions when chastised about walking around the bay house with nothing on but loose and well-worn boxer drawers
2. also referred to, solely by old Mush himself, as 'dead skin'

Example: **deep breath* Hey, Mush! Better put some pants on. We've got company. To which he'd reply, "Dead bird never falls out of its nest."*

duskin' – v. [DUSK-in]

1. the act of hunting waterfowl unlawfully after sunset
2. an illegal activity made popular in the latter half of the nineteenth century from which were created many modern regulations associated with hunting ducks and waterfowl preservation in general

Example: *You were probably out duskin' when you shot that bird.*

duskin' cork – n. [DUSK-in kawrk]

1. a device made of a wine or whiskey bottle cork, attached to the end of a shotgun barrel with a rubber band, used for aiming at waterfowl in low light conditions
2. an illegal gadget used to hunt waterfowl after permissible hours

Example: *Hey, you better bring your duskin' cork if you're going out this late.*

dysentery – n. [DIS-in-tare-ee]
1. a worm-ridden, well-used publication typically placed upon a shelf and served as the only reference book at the bay house
2. also called a 'dictionary' by most people
3. a book rarely used, if ever, as can be attested by this glossary

Example: *Grab the dysentery down so's I can look up how to spell dictionary.*

eguardo – n. [eg-WAR-doh]
a baseball-sized piece of marsh, spongy in texture, ripped off from the bank and thrown violently at an opponent in a game bearing its name, 'Eguardo Fights'

Example: *The first rule of eguardo fights is to never tell anyone about eguardo fights. They'll think you're crazy.*

fahamsammich – [fuh-HAM-sam-itch]
1. emphatic swear word used when the speaker intends to draw additional attention to something considered to be worth paying attention to
2. term coined by John "Jack" E. Combs Jr.

Example: *Who the fahamsammich ate all the brownie corners and pudding skin?*

good eel better – i. [good eel bet-er]
often mispronounced and more often misheard saying attributed to John E. Combs Sr. when attempting to say 'good deal better'

Example: *You know, using those 2 x heavies made the deck a good eel better.*

gwock – n. [gwok]
1. any number of species of shore birds, typically with long necks and legs, that produce loud calls when frightened

from their resting spots

2. known as herons and egrets to most others

Example: *A gwock bird scared the hell out of me when jump shootin' out back.*

hawk – n. [hawk]

a strong westerly wind often brought about by asking out loud for a little wind (see 'never ask for a little wind'); named for the screeching sound it sometimes produces

Example: *The hawk's blowin' a gale out there. To which the reply would be, "Someone must've asked for a little wind."*

jacking – v. [jak-ing]

the act of using a fixed light, typically one that burns with white gas (see 'white gas') to capture crabs with a net, or eels and flatfish with a spear, both attached to the end of long pushing pole and thrust from the bow of a flat-bottomed boat over shallow water at night

Example: *While jacking last night at the edge of the sandbar, I speared a doormat fluke.*

keynal – n. [kee-nal]

1. any manmade body of water used as a conduit for marine transportation such as boats or Styrofoam rafts

2. called a 'canal' by most people

Example: *I was crabbing along the bulkhead in the keynal on the way in, and a gwock bird scared the daylights out of me.*

lemonade stand – n. [lem-uh-neyd stand]

constructed cheaply and quickly, and too close to the bay house to be functional, a small duck blind made of gardening stakes and burlap cloth

Example: *No wonder you didn't shoot any birds. You were sitting in that lemonade stand all morning drinkin' apricot brandy and crème de menthe.*

load up – v. [lohd uhp]

1. the act of a hunting or other dog jumping into a vehicle such as a boat or car to initiate transportation to another location
2. n. the call made to initiate the desire for a dog to jump into a vehicle

Example: *Time to go! Load up, Turk!*

metahen – n. [met-uh-hen]
1. any bird making unusual sounds from deep in the marsh cricks being rarely seen and often heard after sunset
2. called a 'meadow hen' by most people
3. the American bittern or clapper rail bird species

Example: *The metahens sure are making a racket out there tonight.*

morphydite – n. [mawr-fee-dahy-t]
1. any surgically altered, taxidermied animal made to look as if one completely unrelated species has mated with another to produce a hybrid species
2. an abomination of nature

Example: *What kind of bird did you shoot? Looks like a morphydite between a goose and fish.*

nagel – n. [nay-gul]
any fastening device reminiscent of an ordinary nail (see 'D'agastino')

neck stew – n. [nek stoo]
1. the only dish said to be made from any migratory bird with an exceptionally long neck, such as a mute swan or crane
2. a truly awful tasting dish best served on a bed of seaweed collected at low tide with a side of ribbed mussels and periwinkle snails

Example: *The only thing you can make outta' that is neck stew.*

never ask for a little wind – i. [nev-er ask fer uh lit-l wind]
1. superstitious appellation used whenever someone openly

wishes for a breeze to either provide respite from warmth or insects; inevitably results in arrival of the hawk (see 'hawk')

2. saying attributed to Mush's "Uncle Skinny," an enigmatic character never met by anyone at the bay house, only mentioned when Mush would say, "Uncle Skinny used to say . . ."

Example: *Upon the unintentional slamming of the screen door by a strong gust. "Should've never asked for a little wind."*

one more, no more – i. [wuhn mawr, noh mawr]

an excuse one makes when choosing to stay out at the bay house before heading up shore, specifically referring to an additional alcoholic beverage . . . or three

Example: *Hey, we better head back up shore. To which the other person replies, "One more, no more."*

plenty of water . . . just spread out thin – i. [You can do it . . .]

used as an excuse for accessing or leaving the bay house no matter how low the tide

Example: *Someone comments from inside the bay house, "I don't think he's going to make it in." In reply, another answers, "Plenty of water. Just spread out thin."*

pumpkin seed – n. [PUHMP-kin seed]

a small, one-man, camouflaged, ovate boat used for hunting ducks in low water and narrow cricks

Example: *I'm taking the pumpkin seed in the crick near Sore Thumb Point tomorrow.*

razor blade – n. [REY-zer-bleyd]

1. a small (7 to 8-foot-long) garvey fitted with an over-sized outboard engine, often seen skimming across the surface of the bay at breakneck speed
2. a death trap

Example: *You're gonna get yourself killed driving that razor blade of yours.*

Snake, the – n. [sneyk]

a serpentine natural conduit running through the marsh island north and east of the bay house used as shortcut from Long Creek to Scow Creek and as a protected route for transporting cold children in a blizzard

Example: *You'll have to wait for high tide before going through the Snake.*

somethin' ain't two – i. [SUHM-thin eynt too]

1. a recognition of or declaration of an unexpected anomaly
2. an irregularity in either a device, such as an outboard engine, a physical construct, such as the misalignment of two pieces of wood, or a person's behavior

Example: *Upon the report of someone's vulgar flatulence. "Somethin' ain't two with that chair you're sittin' in."*

Spanish flats – n. [SPAN-ish flats]

1. any brand of cigarettes when sat upon and flattened were still able to be smoked
2. most likely a derogatory term

Example: *Hey, can I bum one of those Spanish flats from your back pocket?*

sure sign of rain . . . straw stickin' outta pig's ass - i. [shoor . . . oh, you'll figure it out]

an insult appropriate for the arrival of anyone smoking a cheap stinky cigar

Example: *Someone enters. Out of their mouth protrudes a saliva-soaked stem of a short fat stogey. In response, typically to just the smell, another says, "Sure sign of rain . . . straw stickin' out of a pig's ass."*

twiffle boids – n. [TWIF-l boy-d]

term used for referring to any small chirping bird on the marsh

Example: *Nothing but twiffle boids flying around the duck blind this morning.*

up shore – n. [up shawr]
1. any location not in the bay
2. any location accessible by car
Example: *What time are you headin' back up shore?*

white birdin' – n. [wahyt BUR-dn]
the act of hunting certain species of waterfowl in the unbearable colder weather months of mid to late winter
Example: *You know why we never go white birdin'? It's too cold!*

white gas – n. [wahyt gas]
any liquid flammable substance used in jack lights and space heaters, often used to start the burnin' barrel in an explosive manner (see 'burnin' barrel')
Example: *This garbage isn't lighting. Go grab the white gas.*

What does it mean to be a *bayman*? The traditional connotation refers to one who makes a living from the bay by fishing, clamming, or hunting. Their long, low, flat-bottomed boats speed by me as I serve as an unmoving sentinel on the bank of Scow Creek. I've watched for three-quarters of a century as they casted their nets for bait and raked quahog clams from the substrate. But I believe the meaning of a bayman to be more encompassing.

To be a *man of the bay*, or even a *woman of the bay*, means to have saltwater in your blood, sunlight in your skin, and mud under your nails. But also to understand the ecological importance of an estuary, to be one with the marsh. Most know how to survive by finding food, fuel, and, when necessary, fun. And know what to do when disaster strikes and how to avoid disasters in the first place.

The bay, formed during the past 5,000 years by the interaction of a rising sea with material deposited by receding glaciers, is a miraculous gift. The very idea superimposing scientific understanding with God's purpose reveals what everyone who visits me witnesses first-hand. It reveals my true purpose for existing: to inspire, to enlighten, to educate, and to play my part in the fate of all who drop by.

To surround oneself with my rustic construct means to be immersed in another world. A world ever diminishing by things like lawn fertilizer, poor navigation practices, and generational diaspora. Contemporaries are distracted by technology and minimalism. Holding on to things of the past becomes less popular daily. And that's what I am. A thing, from the past.

But wait! Aren't I also of the future? For if the new can be taught to appreciate the old, the established, the known, then maybe they will carry on the fight to preserve this precious wild, this quiet respite I call the edge of the marsh.

998 Scow Creek as it stands in 2020, reborn from the ashes by a hopeful generation of caretakers, both for the bay houses and their history and for the fragile environment in which they are allowed to exist.

APPRECIATION

Thanks goes out to these people whose contributions made the creation of this book possible:

John E. Combs III, Michael J. Combs, James D. and Paula Combs, Richard "Surf" Laudman, Elizabeth Stuerzel, Linda Stuerzel, Steven Trimboli, Elizabeth (Stuerzel) Helsel, Linda (Combs) Stuerzel, Cindy Combs, Denise (Schimmel) Layden, Jeffrey "Peachy" C. Keene Sr., Brian J. O'Hare, and Fred Ledetsch.

The following people had their stories collected posthumously in part from audio recordings made by the author and his father, Jeffrey "Peachy" C. Keene Sr.:

John "Jack" E. Combs Jr., John E. Combs Sr., Charles "Charley" William Watson, and George "Mush" Carmen.

To my fellow Christian writers at the Tampa Chapter of Word Weavers International for their helpful feedback and perpetual encouragement.

Jeff Keene II, The Peg Leg Penman, but known in his home town as *Bam-Bam* to his bay and firehouse families, was born on the south shore of Long Island and raised in the Village of Freeport. A product of a Freeport High School education, as well as a graduate from both Nassau Community College and Hofstra University, he has used his experiences growing up at the bay house to inspire and entertain his science students in central and south Florida for over twenty years.

Nearly thirty years on the marsh leaves an imprint that lasts a lifetime. Some of Jeff's first childhood memories come from the bay house. They include the German shepherd of a family friend leaping from the dock into the crick, playing on the deck in the sun with colorful modeling clay his mother brought for him, and being put down for a nap in a small bay house bedroom with sheer white curtains blowing from the summer breeze through an open window.

As with many authors, the art of telling stories was something that must have been hidden within Jeff for many years until being struck by the right influences. His adoration of Jesus Christ motivated him to write Biblical historical fiction novels. But the love of boats, outdoor activities, and the solitude of the bay house are only experienced by a select few. And that source of inspiration drove him to create this memoir anthology.

When not writing, Jeff's passions include spending lots of time with his wife, Andria, and their adult children making new memories and having more adventures exploring the Appalachian Mountains in their Jeep Wrangler, beachcombing along the eastern seaboard, or window shopping on Main Streets in quaint towns wherever they find them. He also enjoys woodworking, gardening, hiking in the forest, hopping over rocks, and trouncing through streams. He loves sitting around a campfire with friends and family watching the sunset and giving thanks to God Almighty.

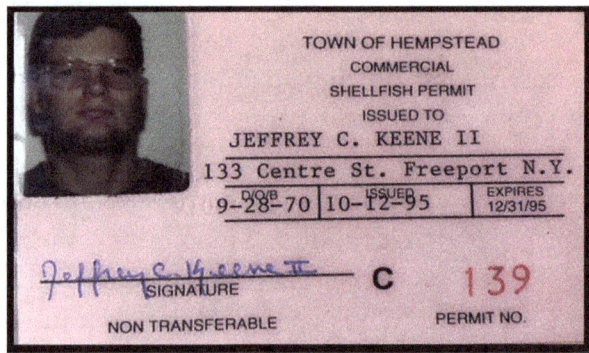

The author's shellfishing permit from 1995.

Pericope: a novel of an adultress

   - book 1 of 3 in the "Go and Sin no More" trilogy

   - published by WordCrafts Press and available wherever fine books are sold

   - released March 2022

   - winner of a Florida Tapestry Award and Christian Indie Award for historical fiction

   Her entire story took up only nine verses (John 8:2–11) of the Bible. We know nothing about her. They brought her to Jesus in the temple as an adulteress. They were going to stone her to death. Before she knew it, she stood free. Her sins forgiven.

   But where did she come from? What was her name? And where did she go after Jesus saved her?

   Follow Pericope as her world falls apart and she believes only death can free her from the turmoil. Does she find an escape?

Yamin: a novel of a demoniac

- Book 2 of 3 in the "Go and Sin no More" trilogy
- published by WordCrafts Press and available wherever fine books are sold
- released March 2023
- winner of a Florida Christian Writers Conference Award

Two-thousand years ago, on the ancient shores of the Sea of Galilee, fisherman and their families cope with severe weather, oppressive rulers, and aggressive rivals in a battle to survive. Yamin, the teenage son of a dying fisherman, must contend with all these trials and being alone . . . for now. His wealthy best friend always had more, and the ambitious young woman Yamin likes wants nothing to do with him. Yamin's jealousy, depression, and self-pity drive him away from all he has known and loved into a dark and demented world. While trying to escape his seemingly cursed life, Yamin encounters corrupt Roman soldiers, revenge-driven pirates on the Mediterranean Sea, and a legion of depraved souls with whom only the Son of God can contend.

Can he come to know peace?

Under the Rainbow

- published by WordCrafts Press and available wherever fine books are sold

- released September 2022

- winner of a Florida Christian Writers Conference Award

A true crime story about the creation, loss, theft, and recovery of a particular pair of ruby slippers used in the 1939 MGM motion picture The Wizard of Oz. The book includes an exclusive interview with a retired Secret Service agent and a foreword from a Fortune 500 company former Chairman and CEO. It also has ties to actress/singer Liza Minnelli, comedian Louie Anderson, beloved Judy Garland, a missing Fabergé egg, and five stolen Norman Rockwell paintings!

When the Other Boot Drops

    - published by WordCrafts Press and available wherever fine books are sold

    - released 2023

A devotional offering hope and healing for those affected by traumatic experiences. The book takes the reader through the authors own challenges as volunteer firefighter whose line-of-duty injury resulted in the loss of his right foot the day after his nineteenth birthday. Keene, a former church Bible class leader and seminary student, shows that both physical and emotional trauma can be overcome so that you can rise to success on the other side.

ALSO AVAILABLE FROM
WORDCRAFTS PRESS

Country Music's Hidden Gem: The Redd Stewart Story
    by Billy Rae Stewart & Gail Kittleson

An Introspective Journey: A Memoir of Living with Alzheimer's
    by Paula Sarver

Deployed with My Mother
    by David Weill & Tammy Chandler

Lean In: Chasing the Sunset
    by April Poynter

Confounding the Wise: A Celebration of Life, Love, Laugher & Adoption
    by Dan Kulp

www.wordcrafts.net

www.ingramcontent.com/pod-product-compliance
Lightning Source LLC
Chambersburg PA
CBHW061802120626
46550CB00005B/2108